MANA GARDENING

EMPOWER YOURSELF
& LIVE A BETTER LIFE

D1178479

MANA GARDENING

EMPOWER YOURSELF
& LIVE A BETTER LIFE

Keti Kamalani
and
Michelle Shine, Ph.D.

MANA
GARDENING®
INSTITUTE
KANEOHE, HAWAII

To our children and all who seek
happiness...

Published
by Mana
Gardening
Institute,
LLC, Kaneohe,
Hawaii Copyright ©
2017 by Keti Kamalani
and Michelle Shine Ph.D.
ISBN-13: 978-0-9961767-0-5
LCCN: Distributed by Itasca Books Cover Design by Mana Gardening Institute, LLC.
Printed in the United States of America on acid-free paper with at least 30% recycled content.
Any non-recycled content responsibly harvested according to PEFC, SFI, and FSC certifications.

CONTENTS

Aloha to You from Us

Michelle and I were research scientists with high-level careers, living in Hawaii, one of the most beautiful places in the world, yet we struggled to be happy. With all we had, we simply did not have the quality of life we wanted for ourselves, our spouses, and especially our children.

As a child, I watched my grandmother hang laundry out in the morning breeze. Without a TV blaring in the background or cell phone interruptions, we heard the birds singing as we washed the tomatoes and cucumbers from her garden. I know that my grandparents worked very hard, but they also lived with a sense of calmness and joy that I rarely created in my own life.

Years ago, Michelle asked how I always seemed happy. Truthfully, I was only happy with some aspects of my life. In a moment of complete honesty, we reflected on being mothers and wives, not to mention primary breadwinners, who desired more joy in our lives.

That day we dedicated ourselves to building happiness in our personal lives. We tried action-based techniques, such as yoga, nutrition, exercise, sports, and faith, all in an effort to live better. We kept detailed notes and constantly put our lives under our own microscopes, but none of our efforts gave us the happiness we were searching for; in fact, we found it a constant uphill battle to be happy. I kept saying to myself, "If it is this hard for us, then how can *anyone* be truly happy?"

Two years into our quest, we were introduced to an ancient Hawaiian concept of accessing a higher wisdom from within, and with this the adventure began! Guided by Master Shen's method of teaching ancient healing techniques, we unexpectedly discovered our own easy way to instantly access that wisdom and positively change our lives for the better.

This discovery took only seconds to minutes of our day, and with it we not only felt happier, we were no longer spinning our wheels. We saw immediate changes without having to go anywhere or sign up for anything. Laughter and playfulness returned, and many of our problems were resolved without an ounce of negative energy.

Finding this higher wisdom flowing within us not only gave us peace with ourselves, it also allowed us to be more intuitive, more compassionate, and more aware of what we really wanted and what we didn't. We had a new energy. We stopped reacting and started reflecting. Our lives became more enjoyable with a new sense of hope and excitement, and we felt happier.

There is a simple way to tap into lifelong inner strength and happiness.

We call this gift to our lives, *Mana Gardening.* The power it gives us, the *mana,* is the traditional Hawaiian spiritual belief of accessing and cultivating life force, and its ability to empower us from within.

As you might expect from biomedical research scientists, a scientific perspective is interspersed throughout this book. Because our personal results were so profound, we share with you a Scientific Prologue containing summaries of the current, fascinating research that provides a basis for the multiple positive results we received from mana gardening consistently. In reading this section you will begin to see why we feel the study of personal empowerment is the new frontier for science, medicine and psychotherapy. In alignment with this, we created the Mana Gardening Institute to implement quantitative studies in physical and mental empowerment, what we define as Mana Sciences™ and Mana Psychology™.

The first part of this book (Chapters 1-4) communicates our story of how mana gardening came to us, transforming us from thoughts of happiness to being empowered to create our happiness. We share how we began using this technique for relaxation and for focusing inward to know ourselves better. These chapters illustrate exactly how to begin mana gardening to feel better in your everyday life.

In the second part of this book (Chapters 5-13), we show you ways to use mana gardening to improve relationships, set boundaries, and make healthy spiritual connections. Techniques for more complex subjects such as physical and psychological wellbeing are also explored.

At the end of each chapter, you will find a *makana,* which means "gift" in Hawaiian. These makana provide you with personal exercises to empower you in your practice. As such, this work shares our journey as well as reveals how to begin mana gardening on your own.

While Michelle and I contributed equally to the creation of this work, this book is written in my voice, in the first-person, to facilitate clarity and avoid the confusion of going back and forth between author voices within chapters.

When Michelle and I looked back at our lives, we realized that we invested two years trying to arrive at happiness, only to discover this feeling was within us all the time, it was free for the taking, and required less daily time than it takes to fold a load of laundry.

With *Mana Gardening* you will learn that you already have everything you need to empower yourself and live a better life.

> True happiness is independent of everything and everyone around you.

Our intention with sharing this simple discovery is that those seeking happiness will discover what we found. Welcome to the journey within.

Aloha nui loa (with much love),

Keti and Michelle

WHAT YOU IMAGINE IS REAL

"Seek first the Kingdom," the Hawaiian healer said to Michelle, but, unlike the rest of the wise souls she encountered, he did not ask her to search for anything; he guided her to look inside to her own personal heaven. That imaginary yet energetic space that is your inner garden is, in many ways, the essence of creation.

What you imagine on the inside can then be created on the outside, in real life. Imagine happiness, create happiness; imagine relaxation, create relaxation; imagine being better at something, and be better at it; imagine healthy, loving, supportive relationships, and have them. Michelle and I saw this firsthand. Our thoughts, visualizations, beliefs, and perspectives profoundly changed our lives, not just emotionally, but physically too.

This series of books was written because of our enthusiasm over what we were experiencing. As biomedical research scientists, we searched the primary literature and sought out what our fellow researchers were uncovering that may provide a basis for the exciting benefits we were receiving from consistent mana gardening.

While this might be a tough read for some, we think everyone will find some useful information. We are delighted to have an opportunity to share these scientific discoveries and trust that the findings reported here will motivate you to enjoy some time mana gardening every day.

In researching the powerful effects of imagination, we came across studies suggesting that what you imagine *is real* on a biological level. Research shows that mental imagery, which is the type of imagining you do when mana gardening, can have measurable, physical effects in real life. These studies have shown how mental imagery affects us in detectable biological ways, such as in brain activation and reorganization, changes in heart rate and blood pressure, and in parameters such as physical performance of tasks.

The first scientific finding we discovered might help those who believe they have trouble imagining in general. It has been documented that those who, at first, demonstrate difficulty imagining, eventually report improved ability with practice.[1] Other researchers were able to document this improvement by showing enhanced brain activation with continued mental imagery practice.[2,3] With practice, imagination can improve! These lines of evidence support the idea that visualizing your inner garden will become easier and easier and may have real effects in your brain.

Many more exciting articles validate the possible physical and psychological effects we were experiencing. Michelle has been a runner since sixth grade and she finds that, besides being great for her body, exercise stabilizes her mood. When she can't make time to work out, she imagines herself trail running in her inner garden; she visualizes herself huffing and puffing up high alpine switchbacks while feeling the exertion of it. After exercising in her inner garden, her mood is stabilized for rest of the day and into the next, just like after she runs three miles in real life.

That Michelle felt better from simulated exercise was very interesting to us, so she searched for and discovered many published studies supporting that imaginary exercising can have real physical effects. Data from numerous neurofeedback and functional brain imaging studies indicate that visual motor imagery (which is imaginary exercising or simulated movement) stimulates several areas of the brain in a manner similar to actual movement.[4-13] Furthermore, simulated or imagined movement and actual movement involve overlapping neural structures in the central nervous system. [1-3,6,13-15]

In one particular study, subjects imagined various finger movements (visual motor imagery) combined with pretending to feel the imaginary movements (kinesthetic imagery). Neurofeedback results showed that the motor imagery of imagining the movement combined with kinesthetic imagery of pretending to feel the movements enhanced the activation in certain regions of the brain.[4] Neuroimaging studies also reported increased brain activation when comparing the combination of kinesthetic and visual motor imagery versus motor imagery alone.[2,5]

Besides just the brain being activated by imagination, studies showed that the body also responds to imagination. Basic vital measurements were taken and recorded while healthy subjects walked on a treadmill. Imagining walking on a treadmill at various speeds resulted in similar changes in heart and respiration rates.[16-18]

Let's relate this to Michelle's imagining trail running in her inner garden. Michelle visualizes herself running up the trail while feeling exerted. Since this type of combined imagery (called kinesthetic motor imagery) has been shown in research studies to create brain activations and body reactions similar to what is seen with real movements,[2,5,16-18] then perhaps this is why Michelle feels better after imagining trail running in her inner garden: her body responds as if she really participated in the exercise.

The mental imagery of Mana Gardening can activate the brain and body as if physical things are really happening.

Being the very active person that she is, Michelle also enjoys surfing in her inner garden. In real life, before she moved away from Hawaii, she enjoyed an improvement in her surfing abilities as her movements became more integrated. She said she finally felt like a real surfer.

In her mana garden, she had been imagining herself pulling off moves she was not able to do yet in real life while also imagining the feeling of the water underneath her board being pushed by her legs as she made turns. Studies suggest that this form of kinesthetic motor imagery added to surfing in real life once or twice per week, may have enhanced her actual surfing performance.

Researchers found that, when learning new tasks, such as dancing steps for the tango, subjects who practiced the steps in their imagination by both visualizing and feeling the movements, for 15 minutes per day, in addition to physical practice, showed expanded brain activation compared to those who practiced only physically. What is more, these subjects also actually performed better than the subjects who did not practice in their imagination.[19] Kinesthetic motor imagery, when used in combination with the corresponding physical activity, can activate and reorganize the brain, and can also improve the physical performance of that activity.[9,20,21] When you imagine exercising and then you perform that exercise in real life, your real-life skills may improve. Toward this end, many athletes now use mental imagery (mentally rehearsing movements) as an important part of their training.[8,22-24] Evidence suggests that the imaginary exercise that Michelle does in her inner garden activates her brain and body, resulting in physical benefits from the imagined experiences.

Massages are another way that Michelle enjoys her inner garden. When she really wants to relax, she imagines getting a massage while enjoying serene surroundings of nature. The kinesthetic imagery of feeling the other's hands on her shoulders progressing down her back gives her senses a treat. She immediately feels her muscles relax in real life as if a massage therapist had actually touched her. We found data to support this too.

Researchers found that the mental imagery of touch facilitated tactile processing in the brain.[25] In other words, the brain reacted to the imagined touch as if touch had actually occurred, suggesting that touch imagined through mana gardening may have real effects in the brain and body. Michelle may have given her body the gift of getting a real massage while simply imagining this experience in the context of her inner garden. Taken together, evidence indicates that imagined experiences cause brain activations and body responses similar to actual events and supports that mana gardening can result in real biological effects.

What you imagine is real on a biological level.

The creation of beneficial psychological outcomes also occurred just from imagining new "memories" in our minds. In chapter 8, I describe how my husband suffered a stroke. He lost many of his memories and, during his recovery, he became angry and frustrated, putting our whole family on edge. After bringing him into my inner garden, I intuitively felt that, if he went to visit his sister and his mother, they could recount their memories of his childhood which, maybe, he would accept as his own.

It worked for him and he returned home with new "memories" from these discussions of his past, which he now felt were his own memories. The perception of having back his memories of his earlier years changed his behavior during this recovery period from almost constant anger and frustration to a more confident and capable view of himself.

Michelle also noticed beneficial effects when she gave herself a new "memory" by replacing a true event with an imaginary event. At one point, while living in Hawaii, one of her dear friends suddenly stopped returning her calls, would not talk to her, or see her. All contact was completely discontinued and the friendship was severed. Although Michelle sought communication and understanding from her friend, there was no response, which, of course, deeply saddened her.

She went about her life and, after a couple of years of practicing mana gardening, Michelle's desire for understanding why their friendship had ended so abruptly resurfaced. Since such communication with her friend had not yet been offered, and asking for it in real life didn't feel right, she decided to give herself the gift of this communication by imagining personal interaction and honesty with her friend in her inner garden.

At a lovely Hawaiian waterfall in her inner garden, she imagined a beautiful, heartfelt session with her dear friend. In her mind (or perhaps her heart), her friend communicated her honest feelings, took responsibility, and apologized sincerely for cutting off their friendship and for the effects this had on Michelle. In this space, Michelle also apologized for her contributions as well as any negative affects her friend experienced.

Although this experience was completely imagined, Michelle felt the emotions of it as if it really occurred, thus changing her perspective and behavior. The next time Michelle saw her friend around town, her behavior toward her friend was more compassionate, less awkward, and less emotionally charged. Michelle's personal confidence and happiness improved due to her changed perception and belief in the imagined experience of resolution.

We found several scientific studies that support the idea that believing a harmless fabrication (such as creating a false "memory" and believing it) can change the behavior of the believer. In one study, participants tried to convince researchers that something false had in fact happened to them. As the participants told the story of the lie, they actually convinced themselves of the lie and started believing it was true as measured using various psychological assessments.[26]

Another research group examined the effects on behavior after creating false memories. The participants in this study were provided with a personalized suggestion (that something occurred to them in the past) or a generalized suggestion (that something occurred to another in the past). The suggestion was either that the participant or some other person had been ill as a child from eating spoiled peach yogurt.

In taste tests one week and one month later involving many crackers and yogurts, reduced consumption of only peach yogurt was shown for those who received the personalized suggestion (that they themselves had been ill due to consuming spoiled peach yogurt). Those who believed the false memory ate the least amount of peach yogurt. This suggests that believing false memories impacts the behavior of the believer.[27]

Perhaps, if you change an unbeneficial memory or experience into a more beneficial one and you start believing it, new behaviors can emerge. These studies support what my husband experienced post-stroke by believing the "memories" from his family members and what Michelle experienced from creating imaginary apology and resolution experiences in her garden that she believed. The behavior of both my husband and Michelle changed due to believing their false "memories".

What if the truth is a painful or traumatic memory? Michelle and I couldn't help but wonder if this method of re-creating experiences via mana gardening could help those with memories of events that were harmful to their personal wellbeing. Perhaps imagining something better is a new way to utilize the brain to restore a healthier self-image.

Until recently, the medical world held tight to the idea that many of our life patterns are set by age three or seven, but neuroplasticity studies are challenging this belief. Science is showing that the mind can still be molded well beyond childhood. (Neuroplasticity is discussed in Chapter 8.)

If it's possible that old thoughts, patterns, stories, and memories can be replaced throughout your entire life, mana gardening may be a far more powerful tool than we thought. What if imagining new outcomes and events in your inner garden and believing them can reduce the power that unbeneficial or unresolved memories have on your personal wellbeing? What if believing the fabricated event or new experience as a memory helps neutralize old emotions and make room for new behavior and thus a new life?

When Michelle imagined in her garden a sincere, heartfelt apology with her friend, she replaced the true experience (that communication had not yet been offered) with a new experience (that her friend expressed her true feelings about ending the friendship). The effect was that Michelle felt a sense of relief and feelings of understanding and compassion that affected her attitude and behavior in a beneficial way.

Jerzy Konorski, in 1948, proposed that if you do not reinforce something that you have habitually reinforced, such as an old memory, and you add a new response or a replacement response, such as a new "memory," or thought, you may obtain new neural reorganization that actually competes with the old memory by inhibiting it somewhat.[28] In other words, if you stop remembering an old memory, add a new thought in its place and continue to think the new thought, new neural pathways can develop that override the old memory and, to some extent, replace it with the new one.

This is consistent with Michelle's experience with the imagined communication, where she felt an immediate shift as if the negative energy of the former memory was gone. She held on to the new perception and new compassionate behavior for several weeks.

However, she later had to go back and "re-remember" the false memory several times to maintain the new perspective, and her belief in the experience, so that she could continue to exhibit the new and beneficial behavior. This effort was, perhaps, reinforcing the new "memory" (instead of the old one) and stabilizing new neural circuitry. Perhaps we will discover that the power of our imagination, with tools such as mana gardening, can give us a way to reset our past, present, and even future.

Along the idea that what you imagine in your inner garden you can create in real life, a month or so after Michelle created the apology experience in her garden with her friend, they saw each other in real life after a yoga class and her friend invited Michelle to go on a hike. Michelle gladly accepted this invitation and, on the hike, received the most openhearted, authentic communication and mutual forgiveness she has ever experienced in her life.

Among the lush foliage near a waterfall (just as in her imagined scenario), in real life they openly expressed their feelings, apologized, and forgave one another completely. Friendship renewed, they both felt as if all discordant energy from the past completely cleared from them. Michelle's imaginary communication and apology experience actually happened in real life.

A similar event occurred in real life after Michelle imagined open conversation and apologies with her then-husband in her inner garden; a few weeks later he took her out to lunch and offered an apology as well. As previously mentioned, this inner garden space is creative, and imagined events have the opportunity to be actualized in real life. This, combined with Michelle's feelings and belief in the imagined experiences, perhaps triggered, magnetized, or opened a door that allowed them to show up in her real-life experience.

Belief is very powerful—it may be one of the most powerful forces to which we have access. The well-known placebo effect has demonstrated the power of belief repeatedly.[29-33] Although other factors are known to contribute to the placebo effect, in the classical sense, it is the conscious belief that something may be therapeutic or beneficial, leading to measurable physical improvement and the lessening of symptoms.

In medical research, this is well-documented with placebo pills, sham surgeries, and the like. Placebos, such as sugar pills, (which contain no active medicinal compounds) are given to study participants by pharmacological researchers as part of the FDA approval program to test the effectiveness of new drugs. Many times, the participants don't know whether they are getting the active drug; however, placebos repeatedly demonstrate equal effectiveness or are almost as effective as the treatment itself.[30,32,34-36] In short, you don't need the medicine at all; you just need to *believe* you have been given the medicine.

Placebos have measurable effects on people: muscle relaxation was produced when a placebo was given as a muscle relaxant and, when described as a muscle stimulant, muscle tension was observed.[36] Intoxication[35] and sensorimotor impairment[37] can result from placebos characterized as alcohol. Compounds perceived as stimulants were shown to have stimulating effects on blood pressure and heart rhythm, and similar compounds when presented as depressants, were shown to elicit the opposite effects.[38] Substances that are not allergenic when presented to study participants as allergens can cause allergies.[34] These results highlight the importance of the patient's belief or perception in physical outcomes. Not surprisingly, the placebo effect has been shown to be related to perception and expectation.[39]

In relationship to the placebo effect, belief and perception appear to be powerful allies in one's well-being. In a 2007 study, neuroscientist Donald Price of the University of Florida and his colleagues used magnetic resonance imaging to scan the brains of patients with irritable bowel syndrome while they underwent a painful procedure.

Price's team showed that when patients believed they were receiving an analgesic, not only did their pain diminish, but neuronal activity also declined significantly in five pain-sensing brain regions and were identical to results in which patients were given a real painkiller.[40]

The patients believed they received painkillers when in fact they received a placebo, and their bodies and brains reacted as if they in fact had painkillers circulating in their systems. This study, and others, suggest that your brain and body believe what you believe.[32,38,40,41] Neuroscience is starting to show that your physical body and your brain react to your beliefs. Perhaps changing your beliefs through imagined wellbeing can create that wellbeing in real life.

Your body believes you; it reacts to whatever you believe.

When it comes to relationships, however, our experience showed us that we had to have mutually cooperating partners at the emotional and heart levels for our imagination, intuition, and insight to create real changes. For example, my intuition regarding my husband, a cooperating partner, increased and our relationship blossomed through my imagined efforts.

In regards to Michelle's former marriage, she could not bring her then-husband back into the relationship, because his heart was not a willing participant. These two diverse situations simply, and importantly, taught us that you cannot manipulate others using mana gardening—other people cannot do what is not already in their hearts to do.

Fortunately, Michelle and I were mutually cooperating partners at the deepest levels and were able to practice mana gardening together through what we call *light gardening* (Chapter 6). Often, we felt as if we were tuning into each other's feelings, emotions, or heart without any conversation in real life. Our intuition regarding each other and our ability to just "know" what the other might need or might feel skyrocketed. These were exhilarating and welcome experiences that inspired us at many levels.

A study involving musicians suggests increased intuition from collective mental imagery. This research study based on brain images and various performance endpoints suggested that when musicians imagined engaging in the musical performance piece prior to the performance, they played well together easily and the music was more cohesive. The authors of the study postulated that perhaps the musicians were tapping into intuition or predicting one another's action or timing to arrive at a more perfected performance.[42]

When Michelle and I experienced increased intuition from mana gardening with each other, we often felt that we were tapping into that stream, that untouchable field of consciousness where we receive information about each other—that same field to which we believe cells are connected. Often, we identically started or ended each other's conversation or started talking on the exact same topic. At other times, Michelle spoke exactly what I needed to hear without a word from me. I was able to sense her when she wasn't around, know when she was feeling a bit off, and give her a call to guide her back to the garden. This holds true even now, thousands of miles away from each other.

Data from studies of the powerful effects of imagination presented here support the idea that what you imagine, believe, or perceive to be true is *real* on both biological and psychological levels. Brain stimulation, measureable physical effects in the body, as well as behavioral changes have been documented based on imaginary events.

Studies in motor imagery (simulated or imaginary exercise) showed that the body actually responds to the thoughts and actions of the mind or imagination. Studies also revealed that the kinesthetic (sensory/feeling) investment is a vital link to neurological reorganization. Psychological benefits are also possible using processes such as mana gardening—if a perception can become a belief that creates a changed behavior and measurable changes in the body and brain, then the field of neuroscience is in its infancy! There is ample scientific evidence to support what we have found for ourselves, that your inner imagination can create changes that will help you live a better life!

MAKANA:

As you embark upon your mana gardening practice, remember that science has shown that your body is responding to what you are thinking or imagining.

This is a tool for health and healing that you may not have considered previously.

PART I

FINDING THE PATH

Chapter 1

Seeking the Kingdom

Early one morning Michelle stood before me enthusiastically telling me about her inner garden. Whatever it was that Michelle was excited about was obviously helping her, because for the first time in almost two years, she looked not only strong and healthy again, but downright fabulous. The clouds of doom lifted from around her; the chains of unhappiness and loss were gone.

I listened with an open heart and welcomed in a moment to learn from an educated woman whom I sometimes taught. And while all my life I have been quick to analyze or discount such ideas from others (I am one of those analytical types and must see everything for myself), that day I felt compelled to listen.

She related to me an idea given to her by a healer who utilized ancient Hawaiian and Chinese therapeutic practices. The idea was simple: you must work things out on the inside before you can work them out in your real life.

"Seek first the Kingdom," Master Shen had said to her. This was profound for her to tell me, because in our years as colleagues I never heard her quote even one word of scripture.

I am a Christian woman married to a Mormon man. Michelle was a nondenominational woman married to a Jewish man. We lived in homes where we had few spiritual similarities, and every day we had to let go of a million differences. Faith was not a common ground in our personal lives, nor had it been any part of our friendship.

"Seek first the Kingdom of God, which is heaven, right?" she asked. "Create that heaven in your mind on the inside and you will have heaven on the outside, on Earth. I will tell you what this means."

She looked great, she was talking excitedly about heaven, and I was intrigued! Being married to a Native Hawaiian man and living on Hawaiian homestead land, threads of heaven or paradise from within seemed to be woven all around me—she had my full attention.

In truth, Michelle and her husband were at opposite ends of marriage—he was letting go and she was holding on. "How do you resolve challenges in your relationship when you are the only one interested in making it better?" she asked me and enthusiastically went on to share her thoughts.

In a session with this healer, he had guided her to create the image of a garden in her mind: a safe, sacred place to ask herself subconsciously what bothered her. This sacred space created in her imagination was what she referred to as *seeking the Kingdom.*

She imagined herself and her husband in the garden, playing and laughing together, without the children. This secret, imaginary garden let her share something sweet with her husband. No matter what she felt about the choices ahead, she needed some truly playful, open, quality time with her husband that he wasn't able to give her right then. I had to pay attention, because there was no doubt this concept was truly working for her. She was all smiles and talking about her husband sweetly.

With this experience, she now saw things differently. She no longer felt the sadness and pain of watching her marriage fade away; she only saw her husband as a dear friend who was unhappy. Her emotions about the entire situation shifted away from negatives and toward wanting her friend to be healthy and whole again. She was empowered from within.

She experienced quality time with him in this inner garden, and it changed her perspective in a way, I believe, she would not have been able to do, nor would have chosen had she tried to adopt a new perspective on her own.

I always felt that having an upbeat perspective was fundamental to holding on to my own happiness, but suddenly watching Michelle transform herself from sorrowful to lighthearted, I made the connection myself:

The only thing in life we truly have the power to change is our perspective.

We shared some of our thoughts on how making a personal heaven or a Shangri-La the starting point for this inner garden concept had not only changed her perspective, but also empowered her to have a positive attitude.

I felt like there was something here we had not been introduced to in any of our studies of healing, meditation, and hypnosis. In reflecting on what we tried in the past, we realized there might be something novel to this ancient Hawaiian idea. But how do you focus inward, let go of your own thoughts, and still find real answers for your life?

With this new concept, she was now guided to make her creative soul the starting point for her to relax and begin her own problem-solving process. Her healer friend, Master Shen, made some important associations that clicked for us regarding seeking heaven on earth:

The Kingdom of God = paradise = heaven =
a feeling of total peaceful happiness.

Michelle had visualized paradise or utopia and put herself there. She made her garden *her* idea of heaven, *her* personal paradise. Visualizing her own paradise as a place in her imagination, within her, made it intensely relaxing and rewarding. The sweetest part was that it took only a few seconds of effort to be transformed.

In her heaven, life was sweetly different, and just by calling it heaven she instantly felt relaxed there. While there, Michelle let go of things easily and recognized her own needs to laugh and play more. What she was saying now regarding her marriage was perfectly aligned with the teachings of Christianity, *Lessons of the Lotus*, and Native Hawaiian ways.

Her new attitude helped her let go of some of her own needs and showed her the principles of unconditional and eternal love. The hurt, the indifference, and the feelings of loss were gone. She loved her friend, who was her husband, more than she loved her own needs from her husband. Her visions of their happiness within the garden had freed her from an unhealthy perspective.

I leaned back in my chair for a few minutes and tried to visualize my heaven. I then realized that I have never given this any thought. I grew up in the Christian faith and had the worldly idea of heaven—white clouds and not much more.

Over decades of personal growth, education, and searching for a closer relationship with God, I never asked myself what paradise would be like for me, or who I would want there with me. It was a simple starting place, and already I felt better just posing this question. I could not help but wonder: *if I gave myself a peaceful place within to enter whenever I needed to feel happy, what else could happen there?*

Michelle and I made a commitment to spend some time considering and imagining our own personal paradise, and at first, we called this *Mind Gardening* because it felt like it started in our minds, especially because our imaginations were involved. Once we started to live it, we realized we were actually accessing our hearts and a higher power within us, which is what the Native Hawaiians call *mana*. In the ancient Hawaiian teachings, power is not outside of us. All power lies within us. We completely felt that power within and it then became *Mana Gardening*.

We started out imagining our own ideas of paradise, our secret and sacred gardens. We agreed to put ourselves into our inner gardens a few seconds at a time throughout our day-to-day lives and meet back in a few days to discuss our experiences. We simply granted ourselves the freedom to enjoy moments within our own ideas of paradise, our own inner gardens, to see what would happen and how we would feel. We had no idea that the journey we were about to embark upon would soon become our lifestyle and would be greater to us than any of our personal efforts or professional accomplishments in science and medicine.

MAKANA:

*What is your idea of heaven, paradise,
your perfect vacation, or your utopia?*

*What is the most nurturing and relaxing space
you can imagine in this moment?*

What do you see there?

*Green mountains, a hammock under a tree,
a beach with turquoise water, a sailboat and a gentle
breeze, a secluded spot next to a stream?*

*Formulate a clear visual image of what your
paradise looks like to you.*

CHAPTER 2

THE INNER GARDEN

What would paradise look like to me? If I were given the total freedom to build a beautiful, sacred, secret place, my own personal paradise, what would I build?

Now, I did not sit down and try to focus on this idea. I simply wondered about it while in the elevator after work, and then again as I drove home. I asked myself about it while I was doing dishes, and later while giving the children a bath. Each time I considered what paradise would be to me, questions arose, such as, *would there be mountains?* Yes, I could see mountains. *Would there be snow?*

Perhaps snowcapped mountains in the distance, but no, I prefer the tropical sun.

I let myself daydream for seconds at a time and began to see paths of flowers and streams of water. This took only a few minutes (if that), and each time I did this I felt happy. I could decompress from my busy life, as if I had given myself a relaxing vacation in what were mere moments of time.

Throughout the next few days, whenever I could steal a few seconds, I would picture myself standing in my garden. And just by beginning this train of thought I was bathed in a sense of peace and relaxation. In my stolen seconds, the garden began to take shape and form; there was no real effort in my attempts to envision paradise, but rather a feeling of taking a deep breath and going along with a gentle flow of thought or imagination. In time, I saw a path that led to a hidden lake.

I thought, *how nice would it be to have a place here by the lake to sit and relax.* In my next mana gardening adventure I saw steps that led to a stone patio overlooking the lake.

I realized that at times the garden took on its own sense of beauty, but I was also able to bring forth everything that I wanted to create there.

Visualize your idea of paradise and allow yourself to be there.

I thought about my garden whenever my life was placed on hold: on the phone, in the elevator, serving someone else's needs, or waiting in line for my turn. The beauty of this on-the-go approach is that it doesn't require setting aside free time. I rarely have time alone or the freedom to take twenty minutes away from my family or work commitments. In fact, I enjoy this technique most of all, because I rarely spend more than two minutes at any given time in my inner garden.

Now, when I find myself waiting for someone or stuck in standstill traffic, I can seize the opportunity for what Michelle calls a mana gardening quickie. Michelle uses the time it takes for software to load at work to close her eyes and enter her garden—and we all know that can add up to hours of mana gardening weekly!

Michelle and I were amazed at the sense of peace and relaxation we experienced, and this sweet sense of calm was only the beginning of the life-changing discoveries we were about to unearth by spending a few moments in our inner gardens.

As often as I could, I would visualize myself seated comfortably on the stone patio by the lake. When I did have a few minutes and felt like it, I would pretend to explore the valley paths that were around the lake. In one of these moments, I pictured myself walking on a pathway and saw two big pearly gates, as if the entrance to heaven. *Ah, I have gates*, I thought. I saw myself walk to these gates several times that day. I felt that these gates were not to heaven per se, but rather the gates to my garden, and I realized that these gates were comforting to me. It was the assurance that I could control who enters my garden—simple enough. *I control my gates*, I decided.

I felt happy from within. With a few seconds of thought, I could feel upbeat and ready to take on any challenge, or I could feel relaxed and at peace. The interesting point is this: there are times in life you really could use a nap, and other times your life is craving a walk in the park. Mana gardening offers me the feeling of either without requiring any real effort or time. When I need to unwind, just thinking about the garden gives me a restful feeling; if I need to feel refreshed, I can explore my paradise.

On one occasion, I pictured myself turning around from inside the gates and gazing back into my garden. There were paths from the gates leading up and down, all going off into lush, green forests.

I used to live in Colorado, but these were not the forests of Colorado; these were paths like those on the island of Kauai—very green, with lots of ferns and tropical plants. As I began walking the pathways, I noticed flowers of Hawaii: plumeria, gardenia, heliconia, and anthuriums.

I kept walking along the path and came into a small cove with beautiful pools, where the water was clear and fresh. Rocks lined the edges of the pools that fed into one another, similar to hot springs that I visited in New Mexico.

In this simple mind walk, I felt overwhelmed with happiness. By visualizing beautiful places that meant something to me, I felt content with everyone and everything around me for several days afterward.

I went walking many times in my inner garden throughout those first few days, and soon I knew my way back to the path that led to the gates. I already knew several of the paths by heart. What I realized was that you only have to visualize snapshots, and when you recall these snapshots, you might notice more details about the picture until it becomes a place you know as well as your own home.

A way to explore this concept is this: pretend you went on vacation to a place you dreamed about your entire life. Close your eyes and imagine you are looking at a photo album or watching videos of your vacation. Be sure to visualize yourself there in the images, laughing and feeling happy.

What does this place look like? How do you see yourself dressed there? How do you feel? You are now *mana gardening*.

Visually walking through my garden, each time I discovered something new. I felt better after thinking about this space; I had my own personal paradise.

And this is another key: your inner garden is a private space, and feeling happy there is a gift to yourself. You can feel free to have everything there as you wish! It is your own sacred, secret garden; a place of pure positivity for yourself.

I discovered that my husband's idea of paradise is very dynamic and filled with beautiful servants! My dear friend has a simple, quiet library she goes to—her dream was not of a large open space but a safe, small, enclosed and special place just for her.

This feeling of paradise, peace, and security is as personal as choosing your own life goals. You are free to have your own idea of paradise. How refreshing! That said, if you are having trouble thinking of a garden or imagining your garden, perhaps you could start with a single room that has furnishings to your desire. As time goes by, create windows and doors and gaze outside them until you know the view well.

When you begin to feel comfortable, leave the windows or doors open. Perhaps you can create a vegetable garden there or an orchard that belongs only to you. You can also use memories of special places you have been as the starting image for your own inner garden. This is your personal, safe, heavenly space.

Michelle explained the concept and experience to me this way: "Creation occurs on the inside first (in the imagination, the mind, or the heart), then bubbles its way to the outside (reality). Imagine a beautiful garden any way you like it. This represents the inside. It is a safe, pleasurable space for you to do inner work. Imagine what plants there are. Is there a gate, a rock wall, flowers, a nice place to relax, a stream, a sailboat, furniture, pillows, a white sandy beach with turquoise water? It is *your* garden, *your* paradise and you can have everything exactly as *you* desire it. Dream it up, bask there, and enjoy that space. In doing so, that happiness you feel will begin to bubble up into your real life—on the outside."

You can enter your inner garden anytime you feel like it—if you are in an uncomfortable space in your real life, if you need a quick break, or even when you feel great. You can bask there for a few seconds or longer and feel amazing anytime you want!

Going there periodically throughout your day can give you more energy to complete your tasks and can totally refresh you. This ancient Hawaiian concept of designing an inner paradise, going there to relax, play or communicate with your inner self, has the power to transform your perspective, and thus your life, in a very quick way.

What was true for Michelle and me was something unexpected. We no longer met to discuss how to *be* happy; we met and chatted about how relaxed and happy we *were*. We had the feeling of being bathed in endorphins, opiate-like substances originating from within the body! If we needed a walk or the feeling of being playful, we did so there in our inner gardens, and if we needed to rest, we closed our eyes and felt as if we were lying in a meadow enjoying a gentle breeze. We felt it was as if the garden wanted only our wellbeing....

MAKANA:

*Take 15 seconds right now and go to
your picture of paradise or utopia and see
yourself there.*

*Actually visualize and feel yourself
experiencing being in that hammock, on the
beach, on that boat, in the forest, in that
peaceful meadow, in the arms of the energy
of love, or whatever scene constitutes your
slice of paradise.*

*This part is really important: make
sure you feel your body relax into the
experience.*

CHAPTER 3

A LIFE OF ITS OWN

Michelle's and my initial experiences with mana gardening were rather like active daydreaming. With each experience we felt a sense of peace we desperately needed in our day-to-day lives.

At first we made things happen there—we orchestrated the events. When we felt the need to be closer to our husbands, we would imagine them in the garden with us enjoying time together. When we needed to feel better about life, we would create ways there to enjoy ourselves. For example, Michelle created the perfect surf conditions and saw herself and her friends surfing glassy, turquoise barrels among the dolphins. Michelle and I saw ourselves playing with our kids on the beach. We often imagined playing music with loved ones in our gardens. If we needed more sleep, we visualized going there to relax in a hammock or sit next to a beautiful tree to reflect on life. In a sense, we allowed our real-life needs to be played out in our inner gardens the way we wished they were in reality.

Then something interesting happened to both of us. Just as we thought we were in complete control of the life in our gardens, helpful events, such as receiving a new perspective, or an intuition about someone, began to occur there naturally and spontaneously. Our experiences in the garden began to flow on their own, often providing us simple answers to some of our real-life needs and concerns. In this relaxed state, we did not have to direct or orchestrate the events that occurred there; our time in the garden began tending to our lives without any effort on our part. We call this organic gardening. We began to feel that we were dropping in on a wave of wisdom and energy.

Some might say we were simply meditating, but for us, time in the garden gave us far more than what either of us had experienced through meditation. While Michelle and I believe there is immense value to traditional meditation (and proven health benefits), neither of us had yet made meditation a daily practice. Setting aside a minimum of 20 uninterrupted minutes that real meditation requires was hard to fit into my schedule and still is. Michelle really wanted to quiet her active mind and repeatedly tried implementing meditation as a practice, but she fell asleep every time, which led to a counterproductive cycle of her establishing and later discontinuing her practice. (That's what happens when you meditate after lunch!)

This seemed to work for us. By visualizing ourselves in our personal paradise, we could let go of everything around us, quiet the thinking mind, and allow for so much more! Entering the garden, even if just for a split second, made us feel good; and it also allowed us opportunities to work from within to create joy or a sense of strength that resonated out into our real lives.

As time went on, the inner garden began to take on a life of its own, and we began to see how a few seconds in the garden accomplished what would normally take us hours, days, or maybe even weeks to do in real life. Our relaxed, happy, clear-mindedness soon proved to be key to solving real problems in our lives.

To understand everything else that will follow in the next few chapters, it will be best to experience mana gardening for yourself. So for now, we invite you to put this book down. Perhaps with the guidance from the previous chapter, you created and felt yourself within your own inner garden, but if not, get excited—creating your garden is a very fun exercise! Take a moment to create, take a walk, or bask in your very own personal paradise, your sacred, nurturing, heavenly space. Then take some time to enjoy it and feel what it feels like to *be* there!

The next two or three times you are tempted to pick up this book, put it down. Take that time to be in your own utopia and bask there even if you have only a few seconds of time. Let your thoughts and visions flow on their own. Simply visualize yourself in your own heaven on earth—your garden within. Above all, remember that the essence of mana gardening is just parking your active mind or imagination in your own personal paradise and experiencing a sense of relaxation within you. The rest will come naturally.

We importantly offer this advice: do not invite negativity into your sacred inner garden. As this is your personal paradise, be sure to keep it pure from discordant energies and only allow positive, feel-good energies there. Be diligent about this and your garden will take on a life of its own benefitting you in amazing ways.

Once you are comfortable with the image of your own inner garden and you have spent a little time relaxing or playing there, then return to this book. This is only the starting point on a road to happiness and more.

Let your active mind relax in your paradise,
far from the world around you.

MAKANA:

Try mana gardening for three minutes every day, for a few seconds here and there—while standing in line, doing some dishes, or waiting for an elevator—and picture yourself in your paradise.

Close your eyes, take a deep breath, and feel yourself sink in and relax. Bask and enjoy that moment.

Begin to notice what occurs spontaneously.

Also try to practice with your eyes open. This is a great skill we call on-the-go meditation, and it allows you to experience the benefits anywhere.

CHAPTER 4

SHARING PARADISE

Welcome back!

Now, come with me on a little walk. I have a place in my inner garden I want to show you: there is a beautiful lake with a large stone patio and a white canopy covering. There are big, white overstuffed chairs with soft pillows where I like to sit in the warmth of the afternoon sun. This is where I like to visualize bringing friends and loved ones into my garden whenever I want or need to talk to them.

Let me ask you if at any time relaxing in your inner garden, did you have a vision of another person sharing your garden? If not, don't worry, just read on! For Michelle and me, the people who first appeared were our husbands. It seemed natural for our thoughts to drift toward them, as part of our desire was to be happier in our marriages.

Mana gardening gave us a chance to feel moments of happiness with our husbands. For me, this was time alone with my husband that was difficult to create in real life. He and I both have custody of our children from former marriages, and we both have big families, which, when we got together, became a very large family of his, mine, and later, ours. With these children came ex-spouses, along with all their added issues and opinions. So, having time alone was often hard to find.

By visualizing that he and I had time together alone, even for seconds in my garden, I felt more content when I was actually with him. My attitude became more fun, relaxed, and open to him when we did share time together. I had more energy to stay up a bit later, and his response to my efforts and openness was not only sweet, but also he was excited, because he felt that we were trying to make time for each other. Although these moments of inner happiness may not be equal to time spent in real life, mana gardening with your significant other can give you a perspective of intimacy and happiness that flows outward into your real life.

One night, I was pleasantly surprised when my husband drew a tub of water and suggested we rub one another's feet while bathing. Getting into the tub, he mentioned my new playfulness and asked me what was up.

I felt relaxed and started chatting away about mana gardening. I told him about some of the experiences I had envisioned of him and me playing in my inner garden, and he laughed.

He was surprised that I had been doing this, and I explained to him that I did so only for a few seconds while driving home from work. He was still laughing, but it didn't matter one bit to me.

Now, this could have been an in-depth conversation, but it wasn't; instead, we were both filled with laughter about how good I felt from visualizing our happiness. He then blurted out, "God, you are a sexy woman!"

I laughed, because this isn't like him at all; he is a man who is more private about what is on his mind.

I felt lively, so I replied, "Oh, you just wait. I am getting sexier and sexier every day."

And together we laughed—we laughed with our whole hearts, and it felt good. And what is more important is that I *did* feel happier, and I *did* feel sexier, which at my age is really profound!

Nothing about either of us was any different, other than how I perceived our relationship after having had some quality time alone with him in my inner paradise.

With that, I changed my perspective to a feeling that our relationship was healthier and stronger than ever. After creating shared playfulness in my inner garden, that playfulness emanated out into real life!

We talked about how in some ways mana gardening is a form of talking to myself and that it did seem sort of crazy. But the truth was that I was finding myself in a better place by starting within to address my need for more time and closeness with him, before attempting to address this with him in an outward way.

I concluded that it isn't really so strange at all to talk to yourself in the inner garden; in fact, I now believe we should all be doing this first. It is far more ridiculous to try to talk out our issues with another person in real life before we talk to ourselves about it and know ourselves from within.

We have a zillion perceptions and assumptions in our heads, and all the emotions that go along with each of them. In talking to someone else, we bring all this junk to the table and usually add to our problems. Without taking time to relax and consider or reflect, it is impossible to know what *we* want when we are talking to another person.

So I told him, "It's probably downright insane that we think we can work out anything at all without dealing with it on the inside first."

Okay, maybe I am really out there now, but I do feel good, I thought. And we both agreed that it didn't seem crazy to either of us, because we were having a blast! We were relaxed, sitting in a hot bathtub of water, rubbing each other's feet with white ginger shea butter. We found it easy to talk about how and why I am so happy and we were being open to our thoughts and to one another in a way that flowed on its own.

I had wanted to be happier in my marriage and decided not to address this with my husband in an outward way. Instead, I went within, to my version of paradise, to solve this, and by imagining us sharing smiles and quality time; in real life I was becoming happier in my marriage.

With mana gardening, we are not telling you that all your problems will be solved or you shouldn't communicate with those you care about. We are saying that if you use this technique to know what you want and visualize it, interacting with other people can be easier.

Perhaps, while mana gardening, you envisioned others in your garden. We discovered that sometimes people appeared spontaneously. Interestingly, we did not feel like we were orchestrating these events or calling forth these particular individuals into our gardens. These images of people exposed us to feelings we had that needed some consideration. It was as if our inner gardens had taken the sole intent of showing us people or situations that for one reason or another, we needed to pay a little attention to.

In sharing our gardens with others, we discovered a very useful tool. When you are relaxed in the garden with

29

the active, thinking mind parked (but not the imagination) and someone appears in your thoughts, you can ask yourself who this person really is to you. In those glimpses of other people, Michelle and I found that our inner gardens can reveal to us those we trust—and those we don't trust at all. In doing this we made some very interesting discoveries.

While waiting in line at the grocery store, as I was enjoying my inner paradise, I saw someone standing at my gate. It was a coworker I had struggled with on some minimal work issues, and I thought in real life that this was trivial to me. But was it truly trivial if he was at the gates to my garden? Then I wondered if I should let him in. Was this someone I would want in my sacred, self-nurturing garden? *No, no. I don't want him in my garden*, I thought, but then I saw myself letting him in.

It was simple. In allowing him to come in and stay close to the gates there was no risk of saying or doing the wrong thing. What surprised me was that by talking to, or maybe I should say reflecting on, this person, these trivial but real issues were disappearing from within me, and I felt more and more that I inherently trusted this person.

In fact, I was intrigued to find out that, in the garden, I even liked him as a person, and holding on to trust within our relationship was important to me. Now, if I were asked in real life whether I cared or if this person really mattered to me, I probably would have shrugged and said I didn't know... but it was clear that my inner self already knew who mattered and whom I trusted. Interestingly, my inner garden revealed to me a feeling of openness and inner trust for him. That is not to say that he cannot sabotage or invalidate that trust with his future actions, but at that moment my inner "trust meter" embraced him.

In my inner paradise, it took just seconds to review the uncertainties of our working relationship that I had buried in my head. Some concerns I didn't actively even know were there. Then, as easy as it was to bring those thoughts forward from subconscious to conscious, I had an awareness of his needs in our disagreement and where he was coming from. All without any of the drama or emotion it could have caused to say even a few of these things in real life.

By spending seconds with him in my inner garden, our conflicts had been resolved within me, and I felt as if we were at peace with each other. Best of all, I felt that I had no need to talk to him in real life about any of it. Any uneasy feelings I had about him in real life were gone. I was free and clear of it.

Sometimes, through mana gardening, you find out you don't have a problem with someone at all. They might have one with you, but your mind can be clearer when you know how you feel about them, or where you stand with them.

In my inner heaven, any time my mind floated to people I had not planned to think about, I asked myself, who this person was to me, did I trust them, and what was the problem? Many real-life problems, people or situations that were making my life harder, or that I wished were different, I could work through in seconds in my garden and instantly know my true feelings.

Perhaps this is the real key: too often we allow ourselves to feel turmoil in reference to other people's actions. This habit drains us of our mana, the personal power that gives us clear-mindedness.

Generally, we have never been taught to organize our thoughts or feelings first—we were trained to be polite and put others' needs or desires before our own, and we do this with people we don't even trust. We were never trained to check in with ourselves first, decide who this person is to us, or to ask ourselves if we trust them at all.

With practice, I felt a newfound sense of clarity with an easy, non-dramatic way to let go of issues I struggled with. In the garden, it took seconds or minutes to clear up what may have taken weeks or months or longer to work out in person.

In person, I would have brought up 10 issues when there really was just one, or wasted energy trying to work with someone I didn't trust or care for. More importantly, I often felt so content by mana gardening through the issue that there was really no need to even talk to the person in real life about it or give thought to the issue anymore.

The next day at work, I physically ran smack-dab right into this same coworker, and he was tender, almost overly gentle with me. Had he changed or did he subconsciously pick up a feeling that I was open to him in an honest and genuinely decent way? Then I blurted out, "You know, I like working with you, and I trust you on a professional level, and as a person too." He laughed and said he felt the same.

The issues I felt, or thought I felt, were gone, as if they had been worked out internally without any real need to work them out in person. *Interesting*, I thought, *coincidence, maybe.* Clearly I understood him better now, because I trusted him as a person, which I never realized before I met him in the garden.

Sometimes, however, you will feel intuitively that the problem must be addressed in person. In those cases, mana gardening may offer you clarity about your needs and feelings, and maybe even some intuition about another that enables true heart-to-heart, in-person communication.

Deciding whether a person should enter your garden is asking yourself to consciously assess how you really feel about them. Remember, your inner garden is *your* safe and sacred space that nurtures *you*.

Regarding others, ask yourself: Is this someone I would want to visit with in my personal sanctuary or live with in paradise? Would I allow this person in only briefly or perhaps require them to stay near the gate? Perhaps, to maintain the serenity of your sacred space, this is someone whom you would want to stay well outside of your garden.

Considering who is welcome and who is not is asking yourself if you totally trust this person. Is this someone you genuinely consider valuable to your life?

As I continued to explore the value of mana gardening, I began to pay more attention to who was intuitively welcome in my garden and who was not. In some ways, knowing the not-welcome list was even more important than I had ever realized.

Mana Gardening reveals how you perceive the people in your life and identifies
the depth in which you value and trust them.

In the real world, we rarely have the freedom to exclude people. We are taught from an early age not to do this. As life goes on we often find ourselves spending valuable time and personal energy on people we really would not want to invite into our lives. Including or excluding people in your inner paradise is based solely on whom you really want or need to share your time with.

Here in your inner garden, you can still love your difficult sibling, but you don't have to feel guilty for not letting them in. The garden is the one place and perhaps the only place in your entire life where you get to truly choose to include or exclude people, and not based on someone else's needs or what is polite.

We are often obligated to spend time with certain people that do not really mean all that much to us on a personal level, such as coworkers, neighbors, and even some family members. Recognizing whom we would not let into our sacred space can make it easier to avoid taking on their problems or needs in real life.

Just acknowledging this freed me up for those I valued, and without any guilt or need to explain myself at all. In reality nothing changed in the real time we spent together; I still listened, nodded, and smiled, but I no longer gave their needs my emotional energy; neither did I take their problems along with me when we parted ways.

The more freedom I felt from this distinction of who this person was to me, the more of a habit it became to assess people right off by asking whether I would allow them into my garden, and to what extent.

One day in talking to Michelle, I put my hands together and made a circular space with my arms and chest. "Everyone who deeply matters to me, who I love and ultimately trust," I said, "is inside this circle. Those I care about or enjoy, or need to work with or interact with that I trust, are on the line of this circle, as if they are on my arms, and everyone else I have placed outside this circle, well beyond my arms, well beyond my emotional wall."

Knowing consciously who was who to me freed from the work it took to manage about 98 percent of the people I knew. (Most of us were raised to never say things like this, but the truth of it was exhilarating!) I discovered I didn't trust my CEO, my HR manager, my next-door neighbor, and several family members, and in knowing this, these individuals no longer affected me personally or occupied my thoughts. Thus, they no longer caused me turmoil.

I'm not saying that I lack sincerity or courtesy with these individuals; I'm saying that I no longer give my power, my mana, away to them. I pass through my moments of exchange with them without giving up my personal reserves of energy. With this knowledge, those beyond my emotional wall passed by me with fewer interactions, and when they entered my real life, I gave them only what was necessary and nothing more.

If people I do not trust appear in my imagination while mana gardening, I visualize asking them to leave my sacred space because I want my sacred space to remain just that—sacred. One profound thing I learned was that I don't need people I distrust to like me; I only have to give to them what's needed for life to run smoothly and effectively.

If you would like to share your garden, we suggest sharing your garden first with those you know you value, those you would without a doubt allow into your personal paradise, those you trust would honor your sacred space and especially, you.

See where this takes your thoughts and imagination. Carry thoughts or images of these special people along with you in your inner garden and enjoy quality moments with them. Perhaps their perceived presence or support will help you relax or change your perspective about something in your real world. Perhaps sharing that space with them will help your relationship feel more special.

If anyone unexpected shows up at the entrance to your garden, somewhere within your garden, or if you just keep thinking about him or her while you are relaxing in your inner garden, consider it your intuition working.

At this point, ask yourself: Do I need to work through something with this person? Is there something to resolve? Do I want them in my inner garden? Is it in my best interest to ask them to leave? So long as you are relaxed and not feeling tense in your body, trust the answers you receive; this is your inner guidance working on your behalf. If you experience stress, then try to simply relax within your garden, and if important, this situation will present itself again.

When an unexpected guest arrives in your inner garden, this is also an opportunity to assess what this person means to you and your level of trust in them by determining at what level you would or would not allow them to remain in your sacred inner space. If need be, visualize yourself walking them to the gates and waving good-bye to them as they exit.

What we found is, with unexpected guests, even after we address them, sometimes they will go away and not come back, but sometimes they reappear at the entry way or even somewhere within our garden without our consent. If they continue to reappear, we ask ourselves why they are there. We try to resolve the issue within our garden without creating any need to confront this person or talk to them in real life about it. Most times after the issue is fully addressed, that person will disappear and not reappear within our inner garden unless we actively choose to bring them in. Follow your intuition on whether or not a real-life conversation is warranted.

Remember, there are gates to your garden and you get to choose who you bring in, or if someone spontaneously appears, whether they exit, or stay in your paradise. This is *your* sacred, nurturing space, and you alone decide who can be there.

MAKANA:

*Enter your sacred inner paradise
and feel your body relax. Picture
a circle and put yourself in the center.*

*Decide who in your world resides in that
inner circle by asking yourself: Do I love
this person? Do I sincerely trust this
person?*

*If so, ask if they
belong in your inner circle. This will allow
you to identify those people who deeply
matter to you.*

*Those you love and trust, who are most
important to you go in the inner circle.
Know the faces of those who belong in your
inner circle. (These faces may change
through time.)*

ENHANCE YOUR EXPERIENCE:

When you find yourself feeling rested, healthy, happy, or relaxed, recognize that moment. Capture an image of yourself in that state via your imagination. See how many times you can recall this image throughout the next few days.

If you see an image in a book or magazine, online or even in a movie that makes you feel excited, happy, healthy, or relaxed, visualize and feel yourself in the scene.

While mana gardening, do not demand or expect silence or quiet. If your surroundings are naturally peaceful, enjoy it. However, it is beneficial to be able to access this feeling of relief from life stress anytime and anywhere.

Learn to enjoy seconds of pure positivity through mini micro moments of mana gardening. Drop yourself into your inner garden paradise for a few seconds. Inhale deeply, experience peace and calm, exhale slowly, and then go on with whatever you were doing.

PART II

GOING DEEPER

Chapter 5

Love Like Never Before

When Michelle and I first started mana gardening, we truly needed to spend more time with our husbands, even though our personal lives at this point were headed in very different directions. My husband was in a place in his life where he was open to me, was working with me, and was listening to me. Michelle's husband had entered a space where he was considering divorce.

By spending time in our gardens with our husbands, Michelle and I were able to visualize quality time with our spouses, giving us both a sense of fulfillment. What we visualized within our inner gardens was what we wanted for our relationships in real life.

In her garden, Michelle envisioned the two of them playing and sharing sweet times together. I shifted my visions from watching the lake by myself to being curled up on the sofa with my husband's arms wrapped around me. Daily, for seconds at a time, I imagined my husband and me there by the lake, snuggling and laughing. In real life, my husband and I became more playful than we had been before.

One day in my inner garden, I created a luxurious bathing area and took my husband there with me whenever my thoughts went to him. That night I felt relaxed about us and did not get upset when he asked me to go to the auto parts store with him and sit in the car with the kids. In the past I would have felt it was absurd for him to even think this was my idea of a nice family evening and I would have made my resentment clear, but instead I just said, "Great!"

Interestingly, it was easy for me to make this adventure fun. I was playful with the kids in the car, I was more open to him, and in turn he was the same way with me. After the auto parts field trip, we got home late and made it easy on ourselves by making breakfast for dinner. We laughed about it, the kids enjoyed it, and rather than being tired and irritable, we were all being silly.

Now, this auto parts night out wasn't at all interesting, but with my happy heart it was relaxing and enjoyable. By mana gardening with my husband before I arrived home, I was happy with him, and we both felt an open and positive perspective.

Later, I got the kids ready for bed and couldn't wait for a real hot bath, but when I walked into the bathroom, there on the wall was a catastrophe. My husband tried to hang a single coat hook, but he forgot there was a pocket door that went into this wall from the room behind it. To rehang the coat hook, he found a piece of scrap wood, painted it, and screwed it into the wall with about five screws. The piece of wood he used wasn't even straight or cut nicely; it was jagged and looked terrible! To make it appear straighter, my husband tried to reposition the wood by removing it from its original spot several times and screwing it in higher.

Added to all this, he tried to patch the holes in the wall, that were the size of a penny each, by making a one-foot-wide swipe with joint compound! Since the walls were textured, the entire wall now looked worse than the piece of jagged wood hanging there.

I said something snotty to him like, "Geez, could you have at least tried to hang it straight?" In that moment all the laughter and fun we shared all evening was lost. The love of my life was now hurt.

The desire of his heart was to do something nice for me with one little coat hook, but now, at 9:00 p.m., all I saw was a bunch of repair work that needed to be done, and that didn't even include the paint that he dripped on the floor.

The moment he turned and walked away, I felt ashamed of myself, and that doesn't happen often. I wanted that happy feeling back, so I tried to park my head in the peaceful feeling of my garden. I then remembered the only thing I can truly change is my perspective. That meant that everything great and fun we had shared that night was in my hands, and I had to be committed to finding a way to laugh around all of this.

I stepped back and tried to find joy in this oddity before me. *I just want to take a hot bath and not deal with any of this*, I thought, *but I can't even close the door without feeling like I need to clean up the mess, and then I have to look at this ridiculous wall!* Back in the garden I went. Relax. Breathe. Simply be.

In the garden my thoughts shifted away from anger. *Would letting go of this right now hurt me?* No, but I could not let it go—it just is not me to let go of a mess. *Okay, then what? How do I get it fixed fast and easy and be happy with it?* I put my thoughts back in the garden.

My husband came back in and started a shower. I held myself in the garden, and I met him with a hug and a different attitude. He was taken back. "Sorry," he said, and I told him to take a shower and that it was okay, we could fix it later. He got in the shower, and I tried to let it go, but there I stood, battling with myself—I just could not let it go until later.

What could I do? As I turned around, I realized that I could hang the coat hook on the back of the bathroom door, which is a solid-core thick slab door. I removed the coat hook from the piece of wood and screwed it into the back of the door. It was that easy—a couple of screws, power drill— voila! Coat hook done, in a few seconds!

Now for the wood behind the door. Okay, down with the wood and out it went to the lumber shed. Then a rag and the paint spots on the floor were cleaned up, and all was done in three minutes! Okay, but now there was a big nasty place on the wall with more than a dozen nail holes. *I wish I could just cover it up*, I thought.

Happy me in the garden replied, "Don't you have some framed art you have never hung anywhere in this house?" So I went to where the art was and flipped though the stack. I came across a beautiful framed scene of water and happy people. I hung it on the wall, it fit perfectly, covered the entire mess, and it looked great! Done!

My husband got out of the shower and found me standing there with a towel to dry him off. I was smiling, happy, and talkative, and then he noticed the art and the hook. Wow! He could not believe it. It was all done, and it looked great! "What about the holes in the wall?" he asked.

"What holes?" I said, and we both laughed. I let go of it (in a way) and this was *huge* for me! I was able to let go of my own anger, I felt a huge relief, and by laughing and being happy, we both felt loved.

"Wanna take a bath together?" he asked.

"Yes, yes, yes!" I replied. And so we did.

What happened the next day was really interesting, too. Driving to work, I visualized my husband with me in my garden again. I could feel his openness to me always, and thought to myself, *king of my heart you are*!

My idea of a king was not of a ruler, but of a benevolent, trustworthy soul who sought out the best for all. And my husband is that man. I hung out in my garden whenever I could that day to spend time with the king and to feel relaxed.

I did not share with him any of this; instead I treated him noticeably differently. I spoke to him as if he was more valuable to me. He started studying the French Revolution and returned to college to study the world in comparison to the Hawaiian culture. We began to have nightly philosophical discussions over red wine and he made time for just us. Perhaps, if you want to be treated like a queen, you have to see your lover as a king.

I was on this path to be happier, and a great part of my happiness was woven into being in love. For this to happen, my perspective had to be locked into the feeling that our being happy together mattered more than anything else.

Michelle's marital situation before mana gardening was very different from mine. Six months after the birth of their second child, her husband announced he was considering divorce, but did not take legal action. They certainly had not been getting along very well, however Michelle felt completely surprised, confused and saddened by this announcement, especially since they were fairly newly married. Michelle took immediate action knowing she wanted to keep their family intact. At Michelle's request, he went to couples counseling with her, and discontinued a few months afterwards. He also went through the motions of dating her again per the counselor's suggestion, showing up physically, yet not emotionally. It felt to her like his heart was not in it. He appeared to be neither *in* nor *out*.

One afternoon, she and I walked into a restaurant where we saw her husband with a young, female coworker standing in line waiting to order food. At first glance, their association seemed date-like. We were quite surprised and when they noticed us, they quickly separated, appearing visibly as uncomfortable as we were. Michelle took him aside and let him know that something or nothing, this behavior felt inappropriate. As time went on, he ended up being assigned to travel with his coworker on several long business trips to Asia each year, and started spending his free time with her when he was back home. When Michelle asked for time to herself, he took their children to visit his coworker.

Although Michelle did not know the true nature of his new friendship, it was painful to accept, and her sadness deepened. Michelle understood that he may need a friend during this time, however, she wanted to be his closest, dearest female friend and it appeared that he was giving that away to his coworker. Consistently offering painful ideas and thoughts, her wandering mind and wild emotions were a challenge to navigate.

Several months later, her husband asked Michelle to stop initiating physical contact with him. She loved this man, and per his request she could no longer touch him. At that point touch seemed like the only thing that could reach him. She felt that they still had a chance because she could feel his heart open just a bit when they touched. With that request, Michelle was heart-broken, and felt completely discouraged. She felt the fear of being alone with two very young children; the thought of her children not having an intact, stable family deeply troubled her. She awoke in the middle of the night to process deep emotions and felt out of control. Her feelings of grief, sadness and failure escalated. She had to deal with feeling rejected, confused, angry and flawed as she continued to go to counseling and do everything in her power to reconnect with her husband.

With the tumultuous emotions Michelle often felt, she still strived to be a positive influence for her baby and toddler. When she was with her children, she focused on them and their needs and enjoyed their presence and life. When she was not with her children, she faced intense and frequent bouts of crying, and it felt like a nearly constant struggle to not be overwhelmed with sadness and grief. She exercised like crazy and did all sorts of things (like kirtan, yoga, hiking, surfing, and singing) to help offset the intense emotions. She often prayed for help and support.

About a year later, support came. Just before an outpatient surgery for varicose veins, Michelle asked a healer trained in Chinese and Hawaiian practices to help her determine whether surgery was in fact the best idea at that time. The veins had appeared years ago, but recently became very painful and were affecting her daily life to a large degree. Michelle, being the type of person who didn't even like to take medication, was hesitant to have surgery and sought out guidance before going through with it.

In the session with this healer, Master Shen introduced her to an ancient Hawaiian, inner garden concept where he had her envision a small, beautiful garden, any way she wanted it. Intrigued, Michelle imagined a grassy area with fragrant white ginger flowers next to a Hawaiian-style lava rock wall. She created that space relatively easily and basked in her personal, imaginary garden for thirty seconds or so, relaxing and enjoying the flowers.

Then he asked her, "What is the first thing that comes to mind when you consider your vascular issues?"

Immediately, she thought of mangoes. At first she was puzzled, then, very quickly, she recognized the message of the inner garden, because she felt she understood what the mangoes represented. You see, Michelle loves mangoes, but she can't touch them. The mango tree is in the same family as poison ivy, and if she gets the sap on her skin she breaks out with an itchy rash.

The garden exercise provided clarification that, perhaps, her increasing vascular symptoms could be a physical manifestation from not feeling free in her marriage to physically express the love she had for her husband. The inner garden concept had brought out this information in a fascinating way that Michelle easily tapped into, without all the emotional pain that surrounded the problem.

Thrilled with the remarkably intelligent and emotionally benign wisdom of this inner garden space, Michelle initiated further discussions with Master Shen that opened her mind to the idea of using this technique to access this inner wisdom in a daily practice. It was so exciting to Michelle to learn of a method that would enable her to use her imagination, relax, and get answers all at the same time!

Master Shen spoke of seeking the Kingdom, the Kingdom of God or the Kingdom of heaven—but not heaven per se, rather her own *personal* heaven. He told her how seeking the kingdom of her personal paradise on the inside, in her imagination, would lead to true happiness in her life. Feeling the brilliance of this concept, Michelle created an expansive version of her own personal paradise, which she then shared with me. This was how mind gardening, as we first called it, came to be.

She started basking in her version of heaven many times every day to have moments of peace amongst the pain she was experiencing. With all that was happening in her home life, she could have gotten lost in anger or depression. While she did experience the intense, raw emotions of grief, sorrow, anger, and jealousy, she did not allow this situation to destroy every happy moment she had as a mother of two beautiful children. Instead, she used mana gardening to give love to herself and others and to envision their happy future.

In her utopia, she envisioned watching sunsets, being with friends and family, and communing with nature. She visualized herself and her husband enjoying quality time together connecting, surfing, laughing, and experiencing a phenomenal relationship. She shared affection and playful times with her children in her inner garden that gave her pleasure and comfort.

To love and soothe herself whenever intense emotions arose, she imagined floating down a mellow section of a crystal clear Colorado River through Moab on a raft while looking up at the red rock canyon walls. With her dearest friends and her children quietly floating alongside her, she felt peaceful. Imagining herself near her favorite high alpine lake in summer in the midst of the abundant white, purple, and yellow wildflowers, she felt the same way she felt when she actually hiked through them years ago—delighted, euphoric, enchanted, and grateful.

When she was ready to let go of unpleasant feelings, she imagined and felt those energies leaving her body and her inner garden, sometimes visualizing them being dumped into a fire pit that would release them. She was able to keep her emotions more upbeat, smoothing out the emotional roller coaster she was riding.

She imagined a golden beam coming from the Divine straight into her heart and continuing to the core of the earth as the light sparkled and twirled, allowing her to feel every cell in her body bathed in loving vibrations. Upon feeling relaxed and peaceful from within, she asked her inner self what she wanted and listened for insight. These rich, inner experiences helped her give and feel love for herself, allowed her to focus on nurturing events that cultivated peace and positive energy, and supported her in knowing herself better.

Knowing what you want allows you to make things better in your life.

After practicing for a while, Michelle's new inward focus allowed her to feel comfortable with her marriage situation for three reasons. First, mana gardening held her perspective toward caring for her husband as a person and away from being angry with him as a wife. Secondly, she was always willing to do whatever it took—counseling, no counseling, programs, no programs, willing to give him space, willing to wait and see. She was *in* and open to the relationship. Thirdly, by visualizing their relationship as solid, strong, and deeply satisfying, she knew all of this was possible for them, if he chose to be *in*.

Although Michelle refused to live in the negative zone, she still cried herself to sleep many nights, and experienced deep emotional pain and sadness as her husband became more emotionally distant. She did not, however, wallow in those emotions day in and day out. She allowed herself to feel her feelings; she sometimes even screamed and cried them out in her car (with the windows up). Upon feeling calmer, she gently refocused and nurtured herself from within, and envisioned things that made her happy.

Whenever her mind wandered to ideas of being divorced or thoughts of reacting, she focused within on something fun or peaceful, or on what she was grateful for, such as her healthy, happy children, her sweet friendships, her loving family, gatherings in nature, dancing, playing music with friends—all that she valued. She did not return the rejection she experienced with more rejection. She simply met herself in the garden, loved herself, listened to her guidance, let go, and always asked herself, "What do I want? Is it the same thing I wanted before, or has it changed?" While facing the most difficult time of her life, she became empowered.

When Michelle looked inward she realized that her heart was completely *in* and she could not choose divorce; they had a baby and a toddler, she loved him, and she wanted to know that she had given her husband, her marriage, and her children every chance to rebuild their family life and thrive. She refused to give up.

With this, she carried hope in her happy heart—either he would decide to love again or he would let go of their marriage completely, but it would be his choice to make. Michelle loved their family and her husband and chose the path to be *in,* love until the very end, and accept whatever came. Michelle was clear-minded about herself and her path; and while that means you know what path you want to take, it doesn't mean that the path will take you where you want to go, or that it will be easy to travel.

What she could not reconcile was the fact that her home life felt dishonest and it was affecting her trust in their relationship. In the early stages of their marital problems, they agreed to keep their private lives private and not share what was happening with their group of friends. As such, most of the people around their lives had no idea any of this was happening. When Michelle and her husband were in front of the kids, friends or family, they pretended to be a happy couple, laughing and enjoying each other, when the reality was far different.

Although these moments of "normal" gave Michelle some relief, this wasn't what she really lived day-to-day. Michelle understood the importance of not creating drama in front of these people. However, as things progressed and got worse, this pretending that everything was great when it wasn't caused her to feel like she was living a lie. It also led her to feel disconnected from any possibility for help and support from friends and family members. She felt isolated, which made the entire situation more difficult.

To be clear, when Michelle used mana gardening to feel better about her marriage, she was playing out on the inside what she wanted in real life on the outside—their happiness and a renewed commitment to keeping it. This helped her feel empowered. When her husband treated her well in public only to reject her in private, it created a sense of dishonesty that bothered her to her core.

She continued asking herself what she really wanted and, in time, realized that the trust she once felt with her husband was disappearing and he lost his place in her inner circle of friendship. She wanted to love her husband, but now, and perhaps more importantly, she realized that she wanted to be loved too!

Michelle got her perspective on! She came to the place where love in the garden meant to love herself enough to go on without her husband. She started doing more things she liked to do. She placed her energy in herself and her children. She used her inner garden to feel strong and confident!

As her confidence grew, she continued to question whether to let this man go and get a new life, or if there was anything else she could do to help their relationship. She was solid, strong, and happy in her own self, but nothing changed in her marriage.

For two years, Michelle went alone to counseling and marriage workshops in an effort to be a better spouse. Finally, a very in-tune counselor that her husband had sought for divorce questions, called him out for being on the fence. The counselor was confident he could help them repair their relationship should they both choose to be *in*.

To love and be loved in a relationship, each person
must be *in*
and willing to let each other in, always.

Her husband was given six weeks to decide whether he was in or out. The counselor knew the immense value of both partners being in. Six weeks later, her husband chose *out*. Since he wasn't *in*, there was no starting point to fix anything. The most fundamental piece of maintaining and repairing relationships—that both partners have to be open to loving each other—was missing. For years, her husband had been on the fence—neither *in* nor completely *out*—and as such he was never truly open to any of her efforts to rekindle their marriage.

Being *in* is being devoted to another and the relationship between you. It is the starting point to building and repairing relationships. The act of saying you are *in* gives energy to the relationship and everyone feels safe, because the connections are not totally at risk. Those who have loving, connected relationships understand that being in is reason enough to celebrate love. You are in, they are in, and you have the opportunity to see the good in one another. You can build, repair, or preserve a relationship that makes you both better people.

Through mana gardening, my relationship with my hubby is the best it has ever been, because he and I recognize the value of just being *in*. As such, we have everything we need to focus on what is sweet and let go of what isn't. None of our added happiness and openness would be possible if either one of us chose not to be *in*.

For another long year, as they prepared for divorce, Michelle faced her husband's almost constant anger and rejection. During this very trying time, she kept herself as happy as possible by mana gardening in her own personal paradise, focusing on everything great in her life, and concentrating on divorce only when necessary to negotiate the terms. When these decisions were required, she asked herself in her inner garden what she wanted so she could make the best choices for herself and her children. Michelle was more empowered to navigate the entire process without sacrificing her personal happiness. Feeling extremely grateful for receiving the gift and wisdom of the inner garden throughout this difficult time, her appreciation soared.

For over three years I watched Michelle love her husband completely unselfishly. I observed her going alone to marriage counseling, and using mana gardening in an effort to navigate her life and hold on to her personal happiness under heartbreaking circumstances.

She placed all her efforts into being a happy person—not negative, not angry, and not bitter. I am in love and am loved, and my husband and I often struggle. She was in love with a partner who was not in love with her, and she waited patiently to give him whatever he needed, even if it meant she had to let him go.

In many ways, Michelle gave her husband a thousand times more unconditional love than I was giving mine. It is easy to love someone who loves you; it's wonderful. But few can share their day-to-day lives and truly give love to a partner who doesn't return that love. She knew what she wanted, stood by it, chose to be happy and love cleanly, without reacting and adding additional pain to the mountain of hurt and pain she experienced. Through this process, we discovered that happiness is not dependent on what you are given. Instead, it is locked into what you give to yourself and to those you love.

Mana gardening, for us, laid a foundation for an increased capacity to love—ourselves and those around us.

We still have to navigate difficult people and troubling situations though. Even if nothing changes in your relationship with another, your own self-love, self-worth, and self-confidence—perspectives that are paramount to thriving—can expand. If you feel like your situation is spinning out of control and that you need help, then seek that, but continue mana gardening to know what you want and to give yourself much-needed peace and love.

When you find yourself in the presence of another soul who chooses to be *in* with you, then take them with you into your inner garden, and laugh and play together like children. Even when they are not beside you, your inner garden will remind you of their great value. Whether they stay in your life or not, even if you give more than you receive, you will have loved with all you have to offer, and this will give you an inner strength, and a sense of peaceful dignity that can never be taken from you.

MAKANA:

Select someone you love from your inner circle. Access your inner Shangri-La and feel your body relax. Imagine your loved one with you sharing some quality time in your inner garden.

Visualize a picnic together, play in the ocean, or curl up together and rest in each other's arms.

Celebrate the fact that this person matters to you and bask in the positive feelings. Later, notice if you feel better about your relationship with them.

CHAPTER 6

LIGHT GARDENING

Michelle and I were amazed at how visualizing ourselves living in our secret and sacred gardens continually renewed us with positive energy. Creative ideas were flowing for us in a way we had never experienced before and we wondered what would happen if we tried mana gardening with each other. Was it possible to become even happier by sharing time in our garden with another soul who wanted to go there with us? What would happen if we both welcomed each other and spent time together, albeit individually, in our inner gardens?

We conducted our own experiment and agreed to go into our gardens with each other and see what we experienced simultaneously. We decided that throughout that entire day and evening, we would visualize spending some time with each other in our inner gardens.

The next morning when we saw each other at work, we had giant smiles on our faces, and when we began to share what we felt and experienced, we both started laughing. It was as if we already knew what we were about to say.

What surprised us was that there were so many identical details in what we visualized independently. The conversational similarities were astonishing as well. We almost simultaneously expressed in real life that next morning that we wanted to write a book on this together, and that the healer who introduced the inner garden concept to Michelle was to share in any financial gain from this. The synchronicity was simply amazing!

We both had clear ideas of what we had to do. We agreed to write down what we experienced with mana gardening, and we realized that, from within our gardens, we inherently already consented to the logistics involved and our roles in working together on this manuscript. How delightful that mana gardening had more to offer us when we did it together!

I began to call this *light gardening* because it seemed almost too easy, as if it assisted us in intuitively knowing what the other person wanted and needed. All of the logistical matters in preparing this manuscript (that we could have spent days debating in real life) were resolved—we were already on the same page without any need for lengthy in-person discussions. That morning each logistical detail we brought up was checked off the list in a matter of seconds.

In addition, the initial framework for this book, and many more books on this topic, were laid out within just a few minutes. It happened so easily that we experienced a sense of relief, awe, and a feeling of sharing a purposeful connection together. It was almost surreal.

When we first started mana gardening, we thought that since we were often directing our thoughts, we were therefore directing the problem solving that took place in the garden. But with consistent light gardening together, we proved to ourselves that this was not the case at all.

In fact, in light gardening, with our focus on each other, we realized we were *not* actively directing the thoughts or the problem solving at all. *Not* directing our thoughts and just allowing the flow enabled us to feel one another's needs. This process was easy, life affirming, and, as we learned later, healing. In light gardening, we simply tuned in to each other from the perspectives of our personal-heavens, and opened to receive insight.

As you start mana gardening, you will likely direct the experience, to some degree, in terms of the scenery and location, but amazingly, after practicing a while, things begin to happen on their own more and more—a shift towards organic gardening begins to happen.

After a while, it is more like you are asking yourself to sit down, relax, and listen (or perhaps watch). It is what the wise have always said: to be happy, you truly have to learn how to let go. It is almost like you are watching a movie as your soul works on things with less and less conscious direction from you, and in doing so, you learn to trust yourself and this guidance, because your subconscious can in some ways make far better and much more informed decisions when you are no longer trying to be in control of everything.

One key concept of light gardening is this: with focusing on the other person and *not* trying to focus on any particular occurrence or outcome, you may discover that you know the people you truly care about far better than you realized. You may also find that they know you better than you think.

In essence, it seemed as easy as opening a gate between our minds or perhaps our hearts. Those moments in the garden, feeling relaxed and in tune with one another, allowed an effortless connection between us to flow on its own.

With our next interesting experiment, we tested the extent to which information flowed between us. This time Michelle asked me to think about her later that day using light gardening techniques. She said she had a reason but didn't offer more—she wanted to see what I would tune in to with regard to what was going on with her—without communicating any of it with words in real life.

What was so interesting about this experiment was that I sensed her feelings and emotional state, but not what was going on with her (her secret). I could sense that she seemed to be actively trying not to spin emotionally. I also sensed that our friendship was extremely valuable to her and that for some reason she was afraid of creating a distance between us.

Later that day, I told her what I sensed in the garden, and, in tears, she told me that I was completely accurate in sensing her emotional state. She told me that she planned on moving away from Hawaii, that maintaining our friendship was deeply important to her, and that she was afraid of losing our friendship, because we would be far apart physically. My senses were intuitive to her feelings. She had nothing to fear because, in my garden, I saw that she was in my inner circle of friendship, and distance does not interrupt that kind of connection.

It was intriguing that I accurately sensed her feelings and her emotional state but not the secret itself (that she was planning on moving). When we met the next day to discuss our thoughts, we simply wrote them down, for we both felt that talking was not needed.

Sometimes, in real life, when we are communicating with others, our feelings and theirs are not accurately expressed, and erroneous conclusions are made due to the tone of a voice or an expression on one's face. However, within the concept of mana gardening or light gardening, it seems the feelings sensed are completely accurate and honest, and these are the most important aspects of communicating anyway.

Michelle was trying to see if it was possible to mind-read in the garden, and we felt confident through this and other inner experiences that we were *not* able to read each other's minds; instead we were polishing our skills of intuition. We both felt pleased that this idea of a mana garden remained a safe place, as it was not corruptible: in sharing your inner garden you cannot give away your secrets to anyone.

Mana Gardening can only show to others what you
truly feel ready to reveal.

Let me explain how I "light garden" with Michelle. I simply visualize myself sitting in a big, white stuffed chair overlooking my lake in my inner garden. There I am and Michelle is there with me. I see her stretched out and relaxed on a white sofa, and there are no agendas or issues. We are simply there. My mind's eye is on the lake, and yet I can feel Michelle, and in these moments I seem to be able to tune into some of her feelings or needs. As I pick up feelings, thoughts cross my mind, but there is no dialogue. If I feel her being uncertain or uneasy, I often realize I already have some idea of what is going on with her.

This is my intuition, and, through light gardening I can access insightful information about Michelle without being in her presence. Michelle tunes into me in a similar way; she focuses on me while relaxing in her personal paradise. Over the next few years, this heightened intuition appeared to facilitate an effortless, flowing connection between us as we shared our careers, our personal lives, and as we wrote together. Our friendship, even though eventually physically distant, continued to grow and flow easily.

Scientifically speaking, on the cellular level, each cell in your body is aware of everything going on around it. They maintain the balance required to do their part in the orchestrated symphony of your existence, *knowing* what to do and when. Each cell generally maintains itself and contributes towards the wellbeing of the entire system.

As individuals, human beings strive for this and fail miserably; we can rarely care for ourselves properly, for those we care about, and take care of the big picture too. How do cells inherently do what's best for themselves and all around them? Is it because they are tapped into a stream of inner knowing that strives for the good of the whole? We couldn't help but wonder if, perhaps, in some ways, light gardening is tapping into that same stream of consciousness or cohesiveness.

Cell biology now had a new perspective for us. We wanted for ourselves the same level of intuitive behavior we saw on a cellular level, and in researching those cellular interactions that happen so effortlessly, we discovered so much more to research and to wonder about! This made us want to light garden even more, and in doing so, we knew intuitively what our common goals were, before we had a chance to talk about them in real life. It made working together and writing these books sweet and easy.

For Michelle, sometimes mana gardening is an active process in which she visualizes hiking, surfing, snowboarding, playing music, or relaxing in the meadow or in the hot springs, and once there, things happen organically. She experienced a gradual transition from directing her time in the garden to organic gardening.

For me, mana gardening is far more sedentary, silent, and without distraction. However, we arrived at the same feeling that the less it was directed, the more healing it became on many levels.

We trust that we may be better off by not consciously trying to resolve everything. Just by placing ourselves in our inner gardens and allowing whatever transpires invites the garden to start nurturing us and working *for* us. Perhaps this is the inner empowerment woven into the stories and songs of the ancient Hawaiians. Interestingly, we feel that we became observational participants in a freely flowing dialogue (or perhaps movie) with the outcome including the best interests of all involved.

In this world, our conscious selves are often on overload and we seem to lack intuition. As we go through our day, our subconscious minds are always on, taking notes from everyone and everything around us like our own personal assistants. Finding a way to use this information that our subconscious minds have stored away helps us make wiser choices and be more accurately updated on everything that is going on around us.

What if you had a security camera viewing your life 24 hours a day, seven days a week, and behind it were 50 well-trained people taking notes on what they saw on camera, 50 people who wanted to maintain your private life and do what was best for you personally? This is exactly what we *do* have within our subconscious mind, but we don't have a way to read our own notes, process them, file them, or use this information properly.

By operating in the way we do in our world today—plugged into the TV, radio, or iPad/iPod, the static and hum of machines and smart phones in our hands and ears almost constantly—our conscious selves are bombarded with so much in real time that we are getting further and further from the ability to use our subconscious recording as a resource of stored data within us. We have become so disconnected from our own intuition that fewer and fewer of us know how to access it anymore.

These became the questions for us: Can mana gardening give us intuition, or perhaps more precisely, can it help us hone this dormant or underutilized skill? Could it be a way to tap into something few seem to have access to? We began to expand our light gardening experiences to understand the process in a deeper way.

In light gardening first with Michelle, I soon felt safe and free enough to begin sharing this concept with other dear friends. One by one, each one of those relationships became stronger, and when we spent time together in real life, the laughter and joy flowed. The feeling of enlightenment was mutual and instantaneous with each. If you have the good fortune of being able to try light gardening with a friend, you may both find your intuition regarding each other becoming more polished.

There was one time when I asked my husband to light garden with me. He is a person who falls silent easily, and I then try to guess what is wrong. This time I asked him to try mana gardening with me so I could see whether I could determine what was wrong, or at least if it had to do with me. He agreed, so the door between us was open, and I found that through light gardening together, I could pick up what was going on with him.

During this experiment, I became aware of his concerns for his children. When I brought this up to him consciously, he was moved, because he had been focused on his children internally. My intuition had accurately picked up on his feelings, and we were able to have a meaningful and brief dialogue addressing his concerns.

What is of vital importance is that, once I keyed into his concerns via light gardening, a doorway opened that allowed honest communication from our hearts, and our real-life discussions took only a few minutes. It could have taken weeks or months to gain the type of understanding I received from mere moments of light gardening.

He felt understood, and we both came away with confirmation that we are in tune with each other and so deeply connected when we choose to explore light gardening together.

Another example of how light gardening assisted me was when I found myself in a strange predicament: I was happy and laughing everywhere except when I went to work. That made me face up to the fact that I hated my job.

For most of my life I have loved my work, but in the shift from medical research to biotechnology business I found myself completely uninspired by the leadership and felt like I was forced to stop caring, which left me despondent. My dear friend Carmen had been struggling with her work too, so we decided to try light gardening. It was in this process of light gardening with her, and realizing her unhappiness at work, that I was able to acknowledge that my own job, no matter how many benefits, perks, or how well-paid, was weighing on my soul.

And then the oddest thing happened to me surrounding thoughts of my job: I laughed. I laughed because here I was wasting my happiness trying to care about a job I didn't want anymore. If I no longer care about my job, I shouldn't be there; it was clearly time to move on. I came to realize how much I needed to quit. It was with this recognition that my perspective changed dramatically.

I felt surrounded by people who seemed professionally dishonest and who behaved like spoiled children. Managers kicking trash cans into the ceiling, technicians having huffing and screaming fits when someone provided constructive criticism, and me, concerned for safety, getting reprimanded for asking people to remove their personal items from the fire exit were all appalling and disappointing to me before. I could now look at the ridiculous behavior with a light heart rather than a critical eye. Each day at my job became funny; it was a riot to be there surrounded by crabby, unmotivated people I wouldn't even want at my funeral. I now saw my work world like a Will Ferrell movie.

Although work became a little more fun for me, it was during this time that several things occurred that were intolerable, and Carmen gave me the simplest answer to all that was going on around me. She said, "You don't want to quit. Tell them to make you an offer to leave."

So I made a list and asked for what I needed in order to move on and have a little time off between jobs. Without her intuition on what I really wanted, I probably would have quit and denied myself the long list of benefits I received, such as my severance package, stock options, the rights to write about my experiences there, and the continued health insurance that would make it easier for me to redirect into my next adventure.

Thankfully, Michelle was with me for the final days of my job, a job that, before mana gardening, was robbing me of my personal happiness—and for that, they just did not pay me enough. Even though it was Michelle who had opened my life up to light gardening, it was doing so with Carmen that helped me fess up to the fact that I was ready to leave my job.

I attribute all of this smoother sailing out and onward to light gardening! By sharing time in the garden with Carmen, the important points were extracted from all of the garbage. In our real-life conversations about our light gardening experiences, we already knew those important points, focused on them, and understood what needed to be done, and this made the entire process incredibly streamlined.

It was quite refreshing to experiment with this and find that my light gardening partner had tuned into my needs, and was able to guide me in a way that aligned with what I was feeling from within. My life was returned to the happy zone, where I was able to laugh about everything around me because my subconscious self and my dear friend already knew that I worked in a mental ward.

We already know subconsciously what we want or don't want, and those who care about us know those same details about us, but we generally don't know how to tap into this stream of shared information. This is another powerful aspect of mana that we would love to research. It seems to us that light gardening with a friend allows us to tap into that stream, providing affirmation of what our inner being already knows. When this happens, we learn to trust ourselves and our friends again, and that makes us feel more ease, greater purpose, and deeper connection.

Intuition is defined as knowledge without reason, or an ability to know something without evidence or proof. Intuition provides us with beliefs that we cannot necessarily justify, causing us to act in a certain way without really understanding why. For this reason, it has been a subject of study in psychology, as well as a topic of interest in the supernatural. The "right brain" is popularly associated with intuitive processes such as aesthetic (creative, artistic) abilities. Some scientists have contended that intuition is associated with innovation in scientific discovery.

In light gardening, you are simply taking seconds at a time to reflect on a person you care about while relaxed in sacred space, and they do the same for you. By visualizing yourself and that person in your garden, it is easier to let go of your active thought processes and feel into one another.

By checking in with that person the next day, you verify what you felt, saw, and thought, and they do the same for you. This affirmation builds confidence in trusting your intuition.

Once Michelle and I started trusting our insight, we relied upon it more often, thus improving our skills and making life easier and more fun. Again, this took only a couple of minutes at a time.

The bonus is that, when someone you trust affirms feelings that you did not share with anyone, there is a huge sense of relief and closeness. When you have a decision you are contemplating, your decision-making process becomes very simple and streamlined when not only do you know what you want or need to do, but someone who cares about you sees it too. This relief, confidence, and call to make plans or take action on behalf of yourself actually makes you lighthearted, and with this change, perhaps, you'll find yourself laughing more at all the crazy events going on around you.

Here is another quick example. You make business travel arrangements, and it is almost impossible to arrive on time for the meeting you are scheduled to attend. You feel stressed several weeks before your travel date. You seem worried, but it's not something you spoke about to anyone. You light garden with a friend, who the next day asks you what all the stress is about. You mention your worries about this upcoming trip. Your friend clarifies what you already knew, but didn't accept—this is not something to worry about. You're now aware of the stress you felt (but perhaps did not acknowledge), and in doing so the stress starts to leave you. Your friend reminds you to simply call ahead and warn the people at the meeting about your time issues. You take action and find out they can move the meeting back two hours.

Did your friend read your mind? No, but they did pick up on the real stress you were giving off that you may have felt, but might not have really noticed or acknowledged. What your friend did was simply bring your attention to the feelings you were carrying around and not dealing with.

In our travel example, your two weeks before the trip are now more carefree. If your plane gets delayed an hour, you will feel relief that the meeting time was moved. When the lady in front of you can't find her driver's license at the rental car office, you won't be bothered or upset; you will take life in stride. You will feel more relaxed, which makes it easier to be patient and gracious.

When you finally do arrive at the meeting, your attitude will be more relaxed and uncomplicated. You will smile easily and laugh openly, because your worries and concerns were identified and understood, and corrective action was taken long before this trip.

Get a trusted buddy and try light gardening together. See if your intuition of one another improves and what benefits it may offer you and your friend. Even if you think you don't have someone to do this with, you can do this solo exercise to improve your own intuitive skills: first identify a few people who are physically nearest in your life. Perhaps choose a loved one, a neighbor, a coworker with whom you share an office area, or someone you share time and space with even if you have no real connection.

Do not ask them to do this with you or share with them what you are doing. This is merely a personal exercise. Then visualize taking them for a walk or relax with them for a minute in your inner garden. Have no agenda. Just feel them, and then imagine you are walking them toward the gates and they are on their way. Perhaps you receive a few details that you need to navigate your life around them better. Perhaps things are revealed to you that you have felt or observed but never gave any real thought to.

Michelle and I did this ourselves and discovered that you can fine-tune your insight and intuition even if you light garden on your own. That grouchy neighbor—you really hadn't thought about it—but after sensing him in the context of light gardening, you get that maybe he is in pain. Your attitude toward him completely changes once the thought *grouch* is replaced by *hurt*. Once that occurs, he unknowingly perceives you differently as well—you are no longer perceived as the busy neighbor—you are now seen as the compassionate person next door.

Intuition creates an understanding that can offer you a way to have more compassion for those around you; nods become greetings, and frowns become smiles. Be sure to understand, however, that these individuals are not *sharing* your garden with you. Neither are you asking yourself to resolve or take on any of their needs. You are simply going to be with them in your inner garden and try to see what you didn't notice when you actually were sharing space with them in real life. Then they are escorted out. With those you love, you can seek mutual benefits, but for everyone else, try to relax and catch a glimpse of them and see what you tune into while keeping your perspective focused on something that makes you happy.

Taking this concept of light gardening even further, Michelle successfully found lost objects by sensing them in the context of light gardening. One day, she looked all over the house for her daughter's beading kit when she remembered that perhaps her intuition could assist her here.

She stopped searching and decided to light garden with the beads. Relaxed in her inner garden, she reflected on the bead kit for a few seconds, and then she saw an image of a school. Then she remembered her daughter had taken the bead kit to school. She saved herself time looking for the beads, and when she picked up her daughter that afternoon, her daughter confirmed that the bead kit was still at school. Her busy conscious mind had no idea where it was, but her subconscious mind remembered!

What we hope for you in light gardening is that, as Michelle and I discovered, you experience your intuitive abilities increasing, you share soul time and deep connection with others, and experience that enlightenment that made us better friends, stronger allies, and true confidantes. May you realize that you truly know your friends on a more genuine level than you consciously realized, and may you share many unexpected and profound organic realizations.

MAKANA:

Pick one person in your inner circle and when you practice mana gardening this week, picture this person sitting next to you in your garden.

Just feel them next to you while you are relaxing and basking in your personal utopia.

Keep your heart and ears open for any intuition about them and if you feel motivated, act on it sincerely.

CHAPTER 7

WEEDING THE INNER GARDEN

Standing in a long line at an airport coffee shop, just off a red eye, I felt exhausted, and still had another long flight ahead of me. I don't sleep well when I travel, I can't get comfortable on an airplane, and I don't rest well when I am away from home. I prefer to sleep on an extra firm mattress, so most hotels leave me with an aching back. Traveling used to be so much fun, but it has become an uncomfortable, overwhelming endeavor of wasted time in crowded lines.

At five o'clock in the morning, as I waited for coffee, the couple behind me bickered loudly, and the young woman in front of me with two small children beside her pushed a worn-out stroller with a crying newborn and a young toddler in it.

I felt pressured by all that was around me, so I made my mind focus straight on the gates of my garden—only this time I saw myself through my gates sitting on a comfortable floating beach chair. I had on sunglasses and a wide-brimmed beach hat. There was a tall glass of plantation-iced tea in the cup holder of my floating beach lounger, and I leaned back basking in the warm sun, floating downstream on calm water. As always the garden reminds me that I can change only my perspective. Thus, the image of floating downstream took all the stress around me and replaced it with a sense of serenity.

With this visual image of floating, I had a simple way to decompress quickly within the garden and let go of the chaos around me. It was this same day that I made a simple discovery about my garden that led to a greater awakening within my life.

Whenever I found my life within my control, I was drawn to sit down in my big easy chair overlooking the lake. Whenever I found my life outside of my control, I was drawn to the image of floating downstream in my oversized adjustable lounge chair raft, letting go.

Whenever the chaos of life is pushing your buttons…

float downstream…

and let it all go.

Later that same morning, I was on a five-hour flight with a very loud little girl, who managed to spend the entire flight kicking the back of my seat. I was clearly in survival mode, because I spent most of the flight floating downstream. The first part of floating always seems to renew my emotional strength, and the remainder of my float makes me feel more rested.

I actually fell asleep off and on in spite of my chair being constantly kicked. I awoke to this child spilling her paints on her mommy's lap. In the chaos of the flight attendant trying to wet a stack of napkins to clean up the watercolors, I went back to my floating beach lounger.

Then, in my garden, I saw this child and her mommy wandering along the edge of the water. Nothing personal, but I thought to myself, *oh no, you two don't belong here!* I knew immediately that, just as weeds can grow in my real garden at home, I might have to learn to pull out weeds that appear while mana gardening.

From within, I politely asked them to leave my inner garden. I explained to them that I needed peace and that my garden was a private place. They went up the pathway and were gone. I arrived at the airport feeling calm and relaxed.

At another time, I had a moment in my inner garden where my boss appeared at the gates to my garden. I knew right away that I did not want him in my garden, but there he was, standing outside my gates.

In real life, I called Michelle and asked her what she thought I should do. I was clear on how to weed out people who had no place in my life (those who pass by our lives on the periphery, but do not truly enter, like the mommy and her child). However, he was a person with power over aspects of my life (as the CEO of the company), and I felt that, perhaps, I should not simply weed him out without even a wave of thought.

In speaking with Michelle, we acknowledged that, perhaps, he and I needed to work something out on a personal level. There were details I observed about him professionally that bothered me and my inner self must have known it would be healthier for me if I felt better about the time I had to spend with him at work.

Michelle and I talked about this in depth, because we had been unsure what to do with people whom we needed or wanted to work things out with, but did not want to invite into our sacred garden space. With our choice to keep our inner gardens sacred and allow no negative energies, we needed some way to work with these individuals without potentially polluting our sacred inner heavens. Michelle suggested I create a place in my garden for sharing with such individuals without actually sharing my garden per se.

As we talked about this, she suggested that I focus my thoughts toward creating a café. Michelle pointed out that this would offer those people who are not within my life or my inner circle to share a view of my garden but not enter it. It would also offer me a space to work with others without inviting them (or their potentially discordant energies) into my personal, nurturing space. Sharing a moment of time in the concept of the café in my garden was for my benefit in letting go, organizing, or clearing up an aspect of my life that was being affected by someone else. Yes, this I could do.

So I got off the phone and as I folded clothes in real life, I entered my inner garden and walked to the gates. There, I asked my boss to follow the path along the outside of the garden to the top of the hill and meet me at the café overlooking my garden.

In my mind's eye, I could see him turn and walk away along the path. I took a different path within my beautiful garden, and there, in a clearing, I came to a lovely Mediterranean-style café with a handsome server asking me if I would like something cool to drink. "Yes," I replied, "A plantation iced tea." He nodded as if he already knew what I wanted. I laughed a bit, because I realized this was also my favorite drink for floating downstream, and a beverage I rarely actually enjoy. It was my own personal café with a single table standing on a patio overlooking my garden where the view was breathtaking.

It felt good to know that this café was there for me whenever I might need to get clarity concerning someone or something. I envisioned the server escorting my CEO to my table as I invited him to sit down with me to talk for a while.

I let my inner self speak to my boss freely. Our café conversation actually flowed on its own. It was revealed to me who he saw himself to be, his values, his life path, and how he thought of himself. All this was going on in my inner café, and then I realized his actions did not match his vision of himself.

He always presented himself as a family man who wanted to see our company also as a family, but our work life was truly the opposite of that. In real life, we were all guarded and distant. Being safe in the café, up-hill from my garden, I expressed to him my discontent with this and my disappointment with the way in which our research activities were managed. We were a biotech science company funded by grants, which entailed a level of responsibility above making money like a business.

I also asked him about something that was often said about him by our corporate financial officer. She often praised him, by telling the staff what a great leader he was, because he knew that the most important rule was that we were all expendable. Just by expressing this in my garden, I felt a rush of relief, as I acknowledged what I knew to be painful for me, but had never really thought through.

There in the garden, I was finally able to speak my own truth (without real life consequences)! This gave me an opportunity to know myself better and let go of my disappointment in his leadership.

Then, as if he were speaking right there in my mind, I could hear him say, "I sold stock in these ideas, and the people who bought those stocks want to profit by them. This, and the fact that I want to be well-paid are what drive me. I have no desire to do research; I want to do business."

In the garden, it was plain and simple; while I love good science, I chose to be happy most of all, and the only way to be content right then, right there, professionally, was to come to terms with the fact that my research, while profound enough to obtain multimillion-dollar grants, was now in the hands of a businessperson, and that changed everything for me. What he said in my garden café made sense for me now. This simple mana gardening conversation allowed me to become aware of *his* side of his own views.

Once again mana gardening had made it clear that the subconscious mind is always taking notes on everything the conscious mind doesn't even think there is time to observe. When the subconscious mind is given time to disclose these notes and observations, we can save ourselves hours, days, months, or maybe even years of wasted time suffering at the hands of others.

In opening our eyes up to the truths we already know, via going within and tapping into our intuition, we can prevent ourselves from making misguided choices, living on misconceptions, and analyzing things that don't need our time or effort at all.

What if I continued to waste effort in trying to be a part of a team in which everyone is expendable, while stuffing my real feelings inside and not addressing them? Even worse, can you picture the outcome of this conversation in real life? I doubt I would have been able to hold myself back from causing a pretty big scene. He was the CEO in my work world and he would never be a part of my personal life.

From this inner café conversation with my CEO I was able to look at my job differently, to acknowledge real truths, good and bad, and then change my perceptions to be happier at work. He had no investment in research; he was looking for something he could sell. He and I were not on the same page. Acknowledging these truths was honestly refreshing. I came to know consciously what my CEO cared about, and I could accept that I had no need to befriend him. I bade this man farewell from my garden café and saw myself pulling him out of my life like a weed in my garden.

Over the next week, I was able to play a similar scenario with others I had to interact with. I started by bringing my coworkers into my garden café to review my feelings about each and every one of them. In minutes of focused gardening I was able to redirect my energy to what really mattered in my job. I let go of personalities and differences that, if given any of my time, would serve only to make my job needlessly complicated. A few people at work mattered, and, in the café, it was obvious they had great value to me.

This active form of mana gardening allowed me to organize my thoughts at work. It was as if I had taken 100 loose threads and let go of 88 of those strands. In the end, I had a few single strands left that really mattered. To do my job joyously, I had to let go of everyone that drained my personal happiness. At work, there were a few flowers, and there were weeds, and now I knew which ones were which!

The weeds do reappear from time to time, but it is very easy to pull them when I know what they look like. When I find myself surrounded by weeds, I simply go into my inner garden, and at first, I float downstream in my lounger. When I feel renewed, I take a few minutes to consider who these individuals are to me in the context of the café, and if I can't find a flower, I pull out the weeds! Weeding visually allows me to release the person, the problem, or both.

In addition to floating downstream when life is chaotic, the visual of day-to-day weeding seems to help me let go of the world around me and within me, and you can try this, too. For me, weeding the garden isn't just about weeding out people with whom I do not resonate; weeding the garden also allows me to weed out my inner thoughts, worries, and concerns that, while perhaps real, serve no beneficial purpose in my happier life.

This technique is not dependent on someone showing up at your garden gates or you bringing anyone or anything into your garden; you can just visualize what troubles you and see yourself yanking out a weed (a person, thought, worry or concern) from the ground to help you let go of what is happening within you or around you, should you need to.

Weeding my garden and visualizing yanking out weeds became my saving grace. I became immune to the actions of weeds! At work, I started smiling all day long, and when I found myself in the midst of senseless drama, I thought, *ah, another weed to pull*! Neighbors arguing late at night, children behaving badly, or exes having temper tantrums were simply weeds that I pulled out and tossed aside, allowing me to enjoy all of my flowers!

My happiness was no longer affected by weeds—I could pull out a weed in my garden and move on with my day. Each day was a new day, and in my garden only the flowers were worthy of my inner energy. Best of all was when a flower grew back in its place; those times a stepchild apologized or an ex actually did something nice, I could feel happy for the new bloom! Weeding the garden became a skill that greatly improved my perspective at every crossroad!

Interestingly, for Michelle, weeding her garden happens more slowly. She initiates conversation in her café or in her garden, says what she needs to say, and only sometimes does she hear a response from the other person immediately. Many times she hears a response later at a random time, but she intuitively *knows* what the response or comment is in reference to. She tends to get information piece by piece.

What is more, she has to stay relatively and consistently positive in her daily life by consciously being present and appreciative of all the good in her life, and by practicing letting go (floating, weeding) while not worrying, obsessing, and analyzing in order for the garden (or her subconscious) to open up to her and give her the information she desires.

Perhaps this is the biggest value of floating downstream first: you not only place your thoughts and emotions in the safe, sacred garden concept, but you are actively relaxed. If Michelle keeps herself positive, organic gardening can occur for her, and she hears what she needs to hear.

So, if conversations with others go more slowly in your own garden or café, do not be discouraged. Just wait patiently with a positive attitude, float downstream until the answers come, then weed as needed and truly enjoy all of the beautiful flowers in your life!

Makana:

*This week, notice when you run into people
or problems that have nothing to do with
you (like bad drivers, unfriendly strangers,
slow computers, and any thoughts
or judgments that accompany them).*

*While mana gardening, visualize pulling
each situation up out of your inner garden
like a weed and placing it outside your
paradise. This practice will help you
maintain your peace and positivity.*

CHAPTER 8

NATURAL MEDICINE

M any positive things were happening for Michelle and me as we explored the concept of mana gardening. Immediately, we had more energy to care for ourselves and those we loved. The more we practiced it, the stronger we felt when faced with problems, and we both felt more clear-minded about the choices we made. Plus, we felt physically healthier than we had been in years. The best part is that it took just seconds to place our minds into our safe zones, rest our souls, and invite in people we wanted to spend time with or needed to meet with.

Going within clarified issues from our everyday lives and gave us an easy way to resolve them on the inside before we tried to work them out in real life. Half the time, we found that just by clearing problems up on the inner plane, we no longer needed to take any further action in real life. The air was clear. There was less and less need to do the mental-emotional gymnastics surrounding any emotional "event."

Michelle used to be a habitual analyzer. She barely slept while going through the early stages of marital distress, because she expended so much energy thinking about her perspective, her husband's perspective, and playing out potential discussions between the two of them. Many nights, her overactive mind startled her awake, and unable to go back to sleep, she lost valuable rest. She was drained of her vital energy and needed pharmacological assistance to stay asleep.

With mana gardening as a practice, when topics come up that seem to want her attention in the middle of the night, she places herself in the garden of her mind, nurtures and relaxes herself, has those important conversations if necessary, and, with a small amount of time and energy, frees herself emotionally and mentally. If these topics continue to arise in the middle of the night, she relaxes in her garden while focusing on her breath. She hasn't needed sleep medication in years.

Practicing this technique helped her reduce the necessity or tendency to analyze situations and allowed her to enjoy life more. "A beautiful transition!" she states. She is more present with far less anxiety because she is no longer completely bogged down in her head, analyzing and spinning.

Those seconds spent resolving issues within our gardens helped us feel emotionally balanced and more peaceful. In addition, it gave Michelle and me more hours of free time than we had before. Emotional healing leads to physical wellbeing in many ways, but we never expected that emotional safeguarding through mana gardening could very well be a system for actual physical healing.

Michelle and I work in the field of biomedical research and have advanced medical science backgrounds based in cellular biology; however, we both have expertise in different areas of cell biology, which means we actually enhance each other professionally by working together. Our similarities in science, medicine, and research gave us the opportunity to solidly explore these concepts and how they can promote healing and wellbeing. Our differences also allowed us to tear apart these concepts from diverse points of view.

In our work life, we considered the basic cellular concepts of healing and wellbeing on a daily basis, and as such, we have shared many discussions on this topic. It is well understood that the human body needs all of its nutritional requirements met, but the fact that it also has a vital emotional requirement has been largely overlooked.

Fortunately, in the last 20 years, this concept of emotional wellness as the balance required for healing has created new frontiers in science and medicine. Michelle and I sought out journal publications on healing and came across the term *neural plasticity* or *neuroplasticity*, by neuroscientist Jerzy Konorski, which we found best clarified our thoughts in simple words as it describes the brain's ability to act and react in ever-changing ways.

To spare you the long, drawn-out scientific details, we discovered and focused on a simple article we found on MemoryZine entitled "Introduction to Neuroplasticity."[43] This article states:

> Neuroplasticity can work in two directions; it is responsible for deleting old connections as frequently as it enables the creation of new ones. Through this process, called 'synaptic pruning,' connections that are inefficient or infrequently used are allowed to fade away, while neurons that are highly routed with information will be preserved, strengthened or made even more synaptically dense. ... In either way, the brain is remolded to take this new data and, if useful, retain it.

This is contrary to the widespread belief that our neuronal pathways were set at a young age and unchangeable from that point on. With this emerging research, it is now thought that the "garden" of the brain never ceases redefining itself, and in some scientific circles, this process is even referred to as being "pruned and newly replanted." Thus, the brain can be transformed time and time again throughout your entire life.

Michelle and I were thrilled with this concept, as we were both beginning to see that, through mana gardening, we had a way to visually rewrite things in our minds. Perhaps we can toss out the idea that minds are shaped in stone by what happens to and around us, and instead embrace the thought that our lives can just as easily be reshaped by new thoughts and images.

So maybe you're scratching your head now and saying, "Oh geez!" so here is a more straightforward version: your brain is storing data like a computer and operates your life based on this information. You feel, react, and respond to everything in your life like a reflex that is based on the data in your brain. It was thought that brain data storage happens without our conscious knowledge and stops on its own at an early age.

What was not considered was that we, as individuals, could reset our emotions, reactions, and responses by simply tossing out stored data and offering new information. What is more, your brain doesn't care if this data set comes from your real life or your imagination. That being true, you can reset your brain to edit and delete anything that makes life harder for you and, with that, redirect your life in healthier ways.

In searching for more information on this, we came across an entire education system being developed on topics around this concept. Early in our mana gardening days, the Pacific Graduate Institute mailed us a flyer for their conference called "Imagination and Medicine II, The Body in Depth Psychology: Healing in an Age of Neuroscience." We were delighted to find out that using your mind and imagination to heal your body was not only the focus of a conference, but also the focus of the second conference of its type.

The next year, we were ecstatic to realize that there were many more such neuroscience/imagination/healing conferences. It appeared as if mana gardening techniques were alive in more people than we knew! We recognized that the process by which we have incorporated imagination into our lives may offer more than an easy method to organize and direct our lives through inner guidance and intuition—it may also be a method for psychological and physical healing.

For example, Michelle and I encountered situations where we had to work through sickness, and we felt by working in the garden we found real answers. One winter, I suffered with recurring bronchitis and pneumonia and was not getting better, so I sat down, brought myself into my garden, and asked myself what was wrong. I told my body that I needed to be well and that I needed to know what I could do to feel better.

The next day I woke up and felt better. I went to work, and as I was working, I felt worse again. *Oh great*, I thought, and I imagined myself back in my garden. The first thing I heard in my head was, *you are allergic to work!*

Wouldn't that be nice, I thought, but no, my inner self was adamant about expressing what was really going on. *Okay*, I thought, and I even said out loud, "Show me what you mean." The next thing I noticed was that, as I was working with one particular chemical, I could not breathe. While working in a Class 10,000 cleanroom (a controlled environment for scientific research with a low level of environmental pollutants) wearing all the safety gear, I theoretically should not have been exposed to many contaminants.

I walked out of the area, and I could breathe again. I thought, *okay, I worked with this chemical for over a year and never noticed this before, but I guess this reaction could just have developed.* I walked back into the area, and I felt fine. I continued to work, and I felt okay, thinking, *hmmm, this is odd; I don't feel sick now.* So I asked myself what was going on, and the thing that kept coming into my head was to pay attention to how I felt. I trusted the guidance and did just that.

I worked as I always did, and then, when I reached out and put my hands on the bottle of that specific chemical—and it was capped—I felt sick, as if just getting a cold. I asked my body again to show me what the problem was, and I went about being busy in the lab; however, just as I went back to one specific part of my work with that chemical bottle near me, I could feel my throat swelling, and I could not breathe.

I immediately walked out of the area, feeling seriously sick. I knew there was no scientific evidence for these cold symptoms occurring by just standing near a closed bottle! I could, however, have been having a serious allergic reaction and there was no way to be sure I wasn't creating this scene, but I also wondered if by empowering my mind and body from within the sacred inner garden space, they were now working together to help me find answers.

I am exposed to literally hundreds of possible allergens in my life—I have a farm and several kids—and yet, through mana gardening, I felt my body was saying *no* to this one product. With the removal of that one chemical from my work routine, I felt better immediately. I should add that the year before this discovery, I had pneumonia three times and bronchitis more than that. By removing this one product from my lab, I had no more respiratory problems.

With this lesson, I paid attention to myself more and took my health questions into the garden anytime I felt symptoms of unhealthiness. Whenever I felt back pain or a loss of energy, I took a few seconds in my garden and invited my body to meet with me there to work on solving the problem.

Sometimes the messages were as simple as words or images of *sleep*, *shoes*, or *chicken soup*, to remind me that I needed more sleep, that those house slippers need to be replaced, or that I needed to make chicken soup from a whole chicken to get all the nutrients my body needed. (Don't laugh; it's amazing what it does for your body and soul!) Michelle and I began to realize that when we paid attention to our bodies from within the context of the inner garden, we found real answers. Maybe by empowering the mind and body via mana gardening, we turn on a tap (or perhaps remove a blockage) to the God stream—to Divine consciousness—and allow that stream, that mana, to flow. We felt physically and emotionally stronger and more in tune with ourselves as the mana flowed within us.

Becoming relaxed on a daily basis is very important to the continued benefits. In this, we want to share some valuable aspects for you to consider as you learn and get proficient at mana gardening.

An aspect of emotional healing is in the art of letting go of drama, pain, or tragic memories. We have all spent many hours of our lives letting thoughts in our head circle round and round until we are physically and emotionally drained. We have all had times when we could not sleep and could not eat. We have all faced moments when love was more painful than beautiful or when we were unable to find peace in our lives.

These moments take from us on many levels; they undermine our present and filter into our future, they affect our physical health, plague us in our relationships, and haunt us in our friendships, often robbing us of our chance to simply enjoy daily life. We have all heard the phrase, "It doesn't have to be this way," which is easier said than done.

We have all had someone tell us to move on or let go, but for some reason we can't or don't, and we pay for not letting go; we pay emotionally, which takes a toll on us physically. All this needless suffering, because we never learned a method that helps us effectively let go, move on, or know what we really want.

I am sure that therapy, long vacations, and spa weekends will accomplish this on some level, but often it is not possible to find the time, money, or opportunity for them when you really need them most! Mana gardening is free and takes seconds, and you can use it every chance you get.

For you to have a picture in your head to help you see what I am saying, take lovely Rene, a friend of mine. She was head over heels in true love, and then was tragically widowed just as life seemed perfect. She is now married once again and, while she feels head over heels in love once again, she also finds herself alone more often than she likes as he works internationally and goes abroad often.

When her health began to make a turn for the worse, she felt discouraged. In talking to her about her relationship, I discovered that she is torn—should she stay married or move on? Unfortunately, she internalized all her thoughts and feelings and at the same time fell sick.

Coincidence, or were these events actually parallel? She found no answers for her ailing health and no relief with any of her prescribed medications. She could make herself numb with pain pills and make herself sleep with sleeping pills, she could shake a cold with antibiotics and wake up with more coffee; but none of that really helped. She focused on organic foods and cut back to one glass of red wine occasionally. She went to bed earlier and still felt tired; in fact, as her new marriage went along, she began to feel tired all the time.

Rene and I talked about her doctor visits, and she wondered if age had simply caught up with her. I told her I was sick and down and out the year before, but had now gone a year without needing a doctor's visit, and that happiness was easier and easier for me to find and hold on to. She wondered what had happened to make my life so easy, so I explained mana gardening to her.

She was intrigued. "Seems so easy," she said. "Solve all your problems from within before you try to solve them in your real life. Funny. It's true, if you don't know what you are really bothered by and if you don't know what you really want, you don't stand a chance trying to work through your life on your own or with anyone else."

So she began mana gardening, reflecting on her life and asking herself what she really, really wanted. She now had a long-distance marriage, and felt overwhelmed with being a stepmom without a full-time partner to rely on. She got honest with herself in the safety and relaxed vision of her own secret heaven. She asked herself some real questions. Did she really resent being alone so much? Turns out, not as much as she thought.

Then, at one point, she forgot to go within first and she reacted. She boxed up all his stuff, pushed it all out into the garage, and decided that was it; she was getting a divorce. She reacted and acted, and then she found herself uncertain again that what she was doing was right, because she really didn't know what she wanted or what was right for her; she just knew she wasn't really as happy as she wanted to be.

She came back to her inner garden. There she sat down, sighed to herself, and decided to stop acting out in her own life before she was sure what she really wanted from within. In her personal heaven, she could speak safely and work through all her ideas and opinions without making any real choices in her life.

She called me a few weeks later and told me that after she had packed all his stuff and pushed it out into the garage, she felt nothing but remorse and sorrow without being sure of herself, and after visualizing herself back in her garden, she was not so sure that getting a divorce was what she wanted.

It was through envisioning her paradise that she could relax, and in relaxing, she soon began to understand herself well enough to know that she wasn't unhappy with her life or her husband or even his being away so much; she just never came to terms with the reality of their lives and what it meant to be far away from each other so often.

There, in her inner garden, she finally asked herself what were the aspects of her new marriage that were the most draining for her. What would she keep, what would she change, and what, exactly, was unacceptable to her? Through mana gardening she was able to get honest with herself first.

In understanding her truth, she discovered that she really didn't want to be a full-time stepmom—she came to realize that she was giving away too much of her personal energy in meeting their life needs. She wanted to be happy with his children, and doing so meant letting their own mother be the one who was responsible for them.

She was worried about how they would feel if she asked them to move back in with their mother so she tried talking to her stepkids in her inner garden, before trying to talk to them in real life. Her intuition led her to feel that they would be fine with their own mom, but that they too wanted time with their dad that was just theirs, and they didn't want her to be unhappy over that. So she gave herself permission to talk to her husband about having his kids live with their own mother, and she raised the point that, when he was in town, maybe he could spend half his time with his children doing things with just them, and half his time with her. It was a compromise for everyone, but it freed her of all the kids' day-to-day needs, which became overwhelming with him away so much.

He agreed and, with the new living arrangements she came to see that she really didn't need her husband to be home more—she enjoyed some time to herself. What she needed was that the time they had together be more enjoyable. She brought him into her garden more and more when he was away, and this helped her feel closer to him even though they were apart.

It was in doing this that she came across the realization that he often resisted going places together when he arrived home. She knew that she needed to talk with him about this in person. When that conversation came up, she was free of the emotions around the idea and simply asked him what would make him happier.

He explained, in real life, that he found it stressful to always feel like his return home had to be filled up with commitments to other people and activities that stole their private time from them. She got real with herself and realized that she made it harder for him to have the time he needed most of all from her. In the end, Rene chose to stay with her husband and made both their lives easier by not doing as much for everyone else and not making him do as much with everyone else.

Not long after that, she and her husband had a chance to take a business trip together and came to visit the island where I lived. She called me and asked if we could meet one afternoon for lunch when her husband was busy. We sat together and she shared with me that they wouldn't be making time to visit my husband and me later that evening, because they had made a new promise to stop overbooking their personal time.

She was happy and looked healthy. I asked her about her health, and she suddenly realized that she had not been back to the doctor for almost three months and had been taking no medicine at all. She felt absolutely strong and vibrant.

She had practiced mana gardening in the midst of feeling sick, in the midst of all the doctor visits, and by determining what she wanted and resolving her problems, she freed herself physically and emotionally from the burdens she created in her life. Mana gardening gave her a way to let go of the worries, resentments, thoughts, and feelings that were not right for her and gave her the clarity and purpose to change her life.

To clarify, I am not saying that all illness is simply psychological and that thinking about it cures people. I *am* saying that the body as a whole and on a cellular level responds to everything we think, feel, and experience.

What is possible is this: that just as we wear ourselves down, we can strengthen ourselves up. Most of the time we don't take the time to explore what we really want or don't want, we don't know our own inner truth, or we ignore the truth from within. Holding on to, or living with, unhappiness in any form always requires us to expend energy, and that wears the body down.

Have you ever just sat and worried? Have you ever spent days wondering what you should do or not do, say or not say? Have you ever gotten up in the middle of the night unable to go back to sleep because your mind was going on and on, entertaining different scenarios of some story about your life or someone else's? Michelle and I call this *spinning out,* and we have wasted way too much time on this in our lifetimes. In the end, things went in directions we usually did not agree with, and we probably had little or no control over them anyway. Not only did we waste a lot of precious time in the "emotional spin," we subjected our bodies to the negative energy of unhappiness; the energy that makes us vulnerable to disease and stalls healing.

Let's pretend that emotional energy has a monetary value and you get 100 emotional dollars each new day. Every time you find yourself spinning out, obsessing or analyzing, losing your emotional energy, it costs you. Disagreements with family, arguments, resentment of life chores like going to the grocery store, and every phone call that you feel obligated to make cost you too.

By noon, most of us are emotionally bankrupt or overdrawn. The day isn't even half over, and yet we're running on empty—and that's without facing the kids' homework, making dinner, or worrying about bills. Every time you deplete and go over your emotional budget, you ruin your immune defenses and run the risk of getting sick.

To guard your health, you must protect your daily emotional bank account. Ancient Hawaiians understood this well, Buddha recognized this centuries ago, and Gandhi, decades ago. We found that with our way of visualizing a heavenly garden and (if nothing else) parking ourselves in our own paradise for a few seconds throughout the day to relax, we could tap into that same stream of consciousness, that divine guidance, that mana, that Buddha, Gandhi and the Native Hawaiians experienced anytime, anywhere, without having to commit to years of studies or advanced meditation.

Interestingly, our method of mana gardening appears to be a gateway to other spiritual modalities that makes accessing ancient pathways, such as meditation, easier. Michelle, who formerly had trouble meditating, enjoys a daily practice of mana gardening, meditation and qi gong.

Back to the emotional bank account: learning to stop spinning in your head, by knowing what you want and how you feel about whatever your focus is, can save you from becoming overdrawn in emotional dollars each and every day of your life. The school wants you to bake cookies for the bake sale, and it feels like too much for you; 10 seconds in mana gardening, and you get the clarity you need to know whether to say, "Sure," or "Nope, can't do it this time." You now get to keep those emotional dollars you would spend on baking goods, and you get to do so guilt-free (because you followed your inner guidance).

Hubby is trying to weasel out of date night this week, and you can't stop fuming about it. Fume no more. Ask yourself in your inner garden if you can let it go this week. If so, do so; if not, say so; and if he blows you off anyway, it's a great night for a movie with your daughter, mother, or sister.

If you spin out on these types of situations, your emotional bank account gets severely overdrawn, and holy cow, you are now headed straight for the flu! If you cut out 10 spins and disagreements, you save yourself a lot of emotional dollars, and you gain clear mindedness, relief, and happiness. This means you're way ahead in the emotional zone, and you're going to feel physically healthier too!

What is really exciting is that you can even add funds to your emotional account with mana gardening. Besides just evening out, you can go into your garden and do something you enjoy for some bonus emotional energy! Go into your garden and relax on the lounger watching the lake, see yourself at a sporting event in your garden, or be at the beach—go have some fun in your garden! Enjoy painting, singing, and sailing or take a relaxing hot bath in your inner garden. In fact, if you get busy and don't have time for fun, the garden is the perfect place to have some quick, seriously great, no cost, imaginative fun! Michelle goes dancing, hiking, snowboarding, and surfing with her friends in her inner garden when she feels the need for fun and cannot work it into her day.

Scientists have shown that emotional environments and emotional stress negatively affects cell health. This may sound hokey, but think of it this way for now: If you had to sit on a Ferris wheel circling around and around, you might be okay for a while, but how long can you circle like that and feel normal? How long before you would start to feel nauseated? If you got stuck on a spinning Ferris wheel for 18 hours, your body would react to fears and uncertainty as much as it would the constant turning motion.

Life stressors do the exact same thing to your body. Emotional spinning is like being trapped, not for just one ride, but 50 or 60 times in a row. Sit up one night worrying about your relationship, your job, money or a sick child, and your body enters that same spin emotionally.

Rene was a simple example of how health is challenged by constant emotional spinning. Her spinning made her question her relationship, which in reality was not the problem. She was exhausted from her inner turmoil concerning her stepchildren. She didn't want to look like a bad person for not taking on their care, but in saying yes, she was sabotaging her marriage and her health.

Once she came clean with herself, she could be honest about what she really wanted. She made some new choices, let go of her worries, and removed herself from the emotional Ferris wheel she was riding. Her energy could then be focused on things that made her feel healthier, and her body could do the day-to-day repair, maintenance, and cellular reproduction that is *vital* to a healthy existence.

Rene healed herself in a way that any of us can. If your body is exhausted or ill, you, too, can take yourself into your peaceful inner garden to relax and give a voice to thoughts in your head. You can let your inner self be heard and let your life be dealt with in this sacred space. Mana gardening can offer you a way to move yourself forward in life, and that may help you regain or retain good health.

The conversations you have within the garden also clean out your head, heart, and soul from acquired junk that can prevent you from feeling happiness. The happiness of having made a decision and knowing what you want or need to do in your life is liberating! Having these conversations with yourself or others is a form of good housekeeping that can be done every day to be and stay healthy and can be done to accelerate the healing process when you are experiencing any form of illness.

Mana gardening can help bring to the surface the issues or struggles that plague our everyday lives; it can also help us resolve those issues in a healthy, productive way. But that's only part of health; you still have to do some work, but once again, everything should start from within. That work is much easier if you empower your mind and body together in your inner garden to build strength.

The strength you receive from your inner garden can also help you help another to heal. For example, a few years ago my husband suffered a bi-thalamic stroke. He came stumbling up to the house unable to see or talk. I gave him two baby aspirin and took him to the ER. They tested everything and confirmed that he stroked out in three places in his brain, and on the scans it looked catastrophic.

In the hospital, I spent a lot of time in my inner garden to keep from spinning out with worry and fear. In time, he could walk, talk, and see again but he suffered memory lapses that made everything hard for him. I was thankful just to have him home and to have him physically capable, and so the memory lapses didn't upset me like it did him.

Within the next few weeks, he became depressed and angry that all this had happened. This wasn't like him at all. My husband is a proud man, so he was adamant that he didn't want our children, friends, or neighbors to be around him like this. He could not remember how to play music, which was a huge part of our everyday life.

When he was afraid or angry, I felt alone and help-less in all that was happening. I felt lost in my fears: *What if he is a different person? What if he can't ever play the guitar or piano again? How am I going to help him? Can I help him at all?* I was spinning out, I recognized it, and fortunately, I had a way to stop myself! The payoff in stop-ping the emotional spin was that my focus went away from sorrow and towards strength; my hubby did not need to feel my fear, he needed to feel my strength and hope!

If I have learned one thing through mana gardening, it is that spinning out emotionally does absolutely no one any good. So, I immediately went into my inner garden with one question in my heart. I asked him in my garden, *What will help you to heal today?* I really did not know how I could help him remember and not feel angry or sad. What I heard was as clear to me as if he spoke the words himself: *I need my past and my own people.* As I have said before, he and I have very different backgrounds cul-turally and religiously, so it made sense to me now that he needed to be surrounded by his family, his faith, and his culture—something I couldn't give him.

I called his mother and his sister, who live on an-other island, and they both agreed that he should come see them to find those lost memories from the begin-ning of his life. I had to talk to him about all these plans, because he was often fearful of even slight changes to our day-to-day routine. I was worried that he might see my fear and be afraid himself, and I didn't want to hurt his pride. I first asked a therapist at the hospital, and she agreed the plan might really help him. Then I sat him down and told him that through mana gardening, I could see that he needed his childhood memories back. I explained to him that I made arrangements for him to visit his mom and sister.

He cried tears of joy. He wanted to go and see them but didn't want to seem weak or needy. He desired this, but was unable to ask for it. In making arrangements to travel, he was happier than I had seen him in a long time, and he even picked up a guitar and played a few songs easily, something he had not been able to do since he suffered this stroke.

Mana gardening put me in a position of strength and guided me to intuitively understand what my husband's needs were. Relying on my education, I would have kept him home with me. I would have stayed by my man's side and taken him to therapy every week for the rest of his life. I would have worked, worked, worked to help this man remember, and we would have both suffered through it.

Instead, I gained awareness of his true needs, and I could let this man go where he needed to go. My inner garden helped me help him. He, in turn, was stronger too, because I agreed with the guidance from the garden and felt confident that memories would flow back to him more easily through his mother and sister. I also knew from within that he could make this trip, go there on his own, and that doing so would empower him to feel in charge of his life again.

These feelings within me came from a sense of strength. I looked at his condition totally differently than I would have looked at it as a wife, scientist, or health-care worker. All because of mana gardening, my perspective was different, and I was confident from the studies on neuroplasticity that the brain can be rewired.

Due to the stroke, my husband lost his images of his past—he lost his mental photo album. I understood that his sibling's reflections of the past would become his new "old" memories. I remembered that the concept of neuro-plasticity teaches us that the brain can replace memories just as easily as it can create new ones.

In this analogy, it doesn't matter whether we have our own pictures, because as we put new images of the past back into the mind, those images become our own. It doesn't matter whose good memories are whose, as long as we have good memories. With his sister and mother he was able to reminisce and share their stories and photos of his childhood, which became his new "old" memories! Getting him through this loss, what looked like crossing a four-mile cavern, now looked like crossing a four-inch crack.

By changing my perspective from one of helpless-ness to one of strength, I had real answers, and my confidence empowered me, which then empowered him. He started healing immediately with that trip, and when he came home, he began to play music again, too. He also began to play songs I never heard him play before. I always approached him with joy over what he remembered even when it was something new, because these songs would now become "our" memories. There was no fear for what was lost or different; we simply rebuilt our past with new "old" memories—some of which were sweeter than before.

Michelle and I could not help but feel that the more we practiced inner gardening, the healthier we felt on both the physical and psychological levels. As scientists we wondered if this could be the basis of what we had read on the subject of neuroplasticity. Was it possible to prune our minds, remove memories that hold us back from being happy, and use mana gardening to stimulate new versions of "old" memories that would help us move forward, let go, and increase our personal happiness?

One afternoon, Michelle and I were discussing her efforts to gain closure from her divorce and move on in a healthy way, and as she explained to me what she had done, I realized that she had in fact used mana gardening to "prune her mind and replant it" by erasing (letting go of) some old memories and replacing them with more beneficial ones.

After their divorce, when certain subjects were brought up, such as dating, Michelle found herself getting emotionally involved in the unresolved issues that were the keys to the end of their marriage. She found that anytime she relived these thoughts, she also relived the sadness that she had suffered over the breakup of their home and family. This was exceptionally hard, because she was mostly happy now—she was doing her regular mana gardening daily yet could see herself undergo a complete transformation from happy to spinning when her former husband wanted to discuss how dating again would affect their children.

From her inner garden, she realized that closure was something she needed, and she knew it would be difficult to move on happily without it. She also felt that it was time to really let him go. Not knowing exactly what closure and letting go meant for her at the time, she continued to ask questions while basking in her personal paradise about what she specifically wanted or needed to be happy about being divorced and their both moving on.

She discovered that she needed to believe—*completely believe*—that her former husband did his absolute best and that he was truly sorry for his part in their relationship problems, subsequent divorce, and the pain she had experienced—as sorry as she was for her part and his pain.

Another thing that mana gardening brought awareness to, was the remembrance of the anger they experienced during their marriage, and this prompted Michelle to educate herself about anger. There are many who say that anger is the way that people cover up unresolved pain. Visualizing herself and her former partner hurting instead of angry gave her more compassion for herself, for her own actions, and for her former husband and his actions in their marriage and divorce.

In changing her memories or her perspective of that time from anger to pain, compassion was now a large part of her viewpoint. With her new better feeling of compassion, she could believe that they both did their best during their marriage and the ending of it.

A few days later, Michelle decided to have a closing ceremony in her inner garden. She created a special place within in her garden that resembled their happy surf house in Baja California, Mexico, years ago. She visualized bringing him in, and there, she acknowledged and apologized for her part in the relationship problems, her mistakes and poor communication, her not appreciating him more, and the words she had said one very important day.

From within, she explained a few things to him from her perspective so she could feel they might both gain clarity, neutralize strong negative emotions concerning each other that continued to plague them occasionally, and clear the air. She offered him an opportunity right then to do the same. She sat there waiting to feel some emotional response, but nothing came.

Michelle often said that, for her, answers or clarity from her inner garden often come days or weeks afterward, but this day she felt it was time for her to do something different. She wanted to experiment with the idea of replacing memories in an effort to feel better about the ending of her marriage and about them both moving forward. Her need for closure was very strong, so she decided to play out what he would say as if he actually did say the words she needed to hear. So she imagined right then that he said everything she felt she needed him to say.

Normally, Michelle waits to feel that she has an authentic or organic response. But today she had orchestrated all of this; she directed his response to see if she could create closure subconsciously.

What was so interesting was that, as soon as she finished the contrived conversation, while still there in her mana garden, an image of his face appeared very close to hers, and she actually did feel as if he himself were saying what she needed to hear and more. She even felt as if a loving embrace was offered from him as well. Imagined or not, this was healing.

Michelle called me in tears expressing that she felt she actually did receive the closure she needed in her inner garden and felt immense relief and happiness. By discarding the old memories of unresolved pain and anger, replacing them with a strong belief that she and her former husband had done their absolute best, and offering and gaining sincere apologies for everything, she felt she gained the closure or perspective she needed to successfully and happily move forward in her life. When we talked, she was excited and looking forward to new adventures. Through this inner exercise, she was finally able to let go.

Because her happiness was so important to her, she gave herself this gift in her inner garden. In reality, her former husband had not faced any of this with her in a truly heart-to-heart way, but in her imagination, they both not only took full responsibility for their parts, but also sincerely apologized to one another.

Believing this, she was able to diminish the reality and believe in the better memory or higher perspective that the situation had been resolved and neutralized. She took this on from within, empowered herself to be free from the spin on this topic, and felt able to move on.

You can erase and replace unbeneficial memories
to strengthen yourself
emotionally and physically.

Interestingly, Michelle had to replay this scene in her garden to maintain her belief in it. The old memory of anger, unresolved issues and disconnect from not having a real life heart-to-heart closing conversation, did resurface. It wasn't completely erased by Michelle's single mana gardening event; she had to reinforce the new "memory" by remembering it again.

It is important to note that Michelle was not deleting the memories of marital anger and emotional pain. Rather she created an experience to resolve that pain from within. And this is how mana gardening can help you as well. We are not suggesting pretending something painful didn't happen as all of your experiences created the person that you are. We are suggesting that mana gardening can be an excellent tool for resolving and neutralizing painful memories, and for gaining the clarity and forgiveness to create ease about moving forward. Gaining a perspective that the situation is resolved and neutralized is healing, can even change your neurobiology, and may help you be happier.

What is intriguing is that a few weeks later, her former husband initiated a conversation where they both acknowledged the past and apologized in real life. This is a good example of how your inner efforts can change your reality—how envisioning what you want or need from within may plant the seeds for it to be created in your real life.

Through these inner experiences, we discovered that using your potent imagination can contribute to psychological wellbeing and increased self love. You can toss out old information or memories that do not serve you in a positive way and offer a new vision that may bring you resolution, restoration, and peace. Resetting your brain by resolving issues within yourself can be a liberating and emotionally healing experience that empowers you.

With mana gardening, you can ask your body to work with you for your own healing. You can determine what it is you truly desire. You can stop spinning and complaining, and allow your body to relax into a healing space. You can also offer your brain new information to give you what you need to heal, and you can gain intuitive knowledge that helps you actually help another to heal.

MAKANA:

*Start mana gardening and
feel yourself becoming refreshed. Become
aware of any points on your body
that hurt, or are sore.*

*Acknowledge these places and put your
fingertips on those points, massaging
gently if you like. Focus your
mind on being healed.*

*The gift is that you have de-stressed and
given yourself a moment of relief. You have
also reached out and touched that place
that needs your attention.*

*Giving acknowledgement and attention to
yourself will allow you to become more
in tune with your body and will foster
better communication with it.*

*Pay attention to those points as you go
through your day and try to tune in to
what may be adding to the stress in your
mind and body.*

CHAPTER 9

WALKING A SPIRITUAL PATH

For us, walking a spiritual path means living in the garden with the Divine, with the power of God or Love. Shortly after beginning this journey within, Michelle and I independently began to experience the affirmation and presence of a benevolent higher power while mana gardening. These experiences were profoundly positive and nurturing.

We did not originally want to write a chapter on spirituality, yet something unseen and very real was taking place in our lives, something we could not ignore. Having struggled in our marriages to balance our diverse religious/spiritual backgrounds, we eventually learned to focus on what we agreed upon rather than differences. Still, religious topics were tenuous at times. As such, we do not intend to tie in any religiosity to mana gardening and these beautiful experiences we shared with the Divine, although we do share our spiritual background in order to provide context.

So, if you want to explore this topic with us, then read the rest of this chapter. If you have no desire to read anything even remotely spiritual, then simply skip ahead to the next chapter.

Before sharing these experiences with you, I want to tell you a little about myself. I was born into the Christian faith and as a child I saw my grandparents get on their knees and pray. I was taught there is a difference between great faith (your own personal experiences with God) and religion (opinions or historical accounts of others with God). I was taught and believe in James 1:27 that states that true religion looks after the widows and orphans of this world and keeps itself pure from this world. I tried to live by this, which led me to adopt several children who in turn made my life rich beyond measure. So, when I began mana gardening, I already felt at peace with God, but I only had limited personal, first hand experiences with God, and these moments in my life were decades apart.

As hard as I prayed, I often longed to feel God's presence in my life. What I discovered through mana gardening is that I could feel the presence of God anytime I wanted! Michelle independently discovered this as well, and our individual experiences with the Divine have given us a new faith.

We began by simply being open to the idea of God, a higher power, the creative force, Love, or the Divine. From there, it seemed to be a spontaneous or organic experience. We independently discovered that we felt this presence in our gardens automatically and it seemed to just simply *be there*, like the energy of universal goodness existing unassertively in the background. Further, when we asked for clarity or guidance, the insight that we were tapping into had the energy of unity or oneness and seemed to only want the best for us and everyone else.

After feeling the presence of this higher perspective, or higher power, we each decided to *specifically invite* the energy of the Divine into our inner gardens, and when we did this, we felt that presence, that energy, immediately!

One day, Michelle told me that she had called the energy of Christ into her garden, because she had felt that, in a spiritual sense, she needed someone she could trust to help her. Immediately after asking Jesus into her garden to ponder his perspective, she felt his presence.

In her garden, she and Jesus sat across from each other on a blanket in the grass near some absolutely gorgeous, fragrant rose bushes. He told her that he was proud of her and gave her a long hug that brought her to tears. Michelle was quite amazed and asked Jesus to support her in her life. She welcomed him, he showed up instantaneously, and they shared a beautiful exchange that left her feeling very loved. Hearing this, I felt connected to Michelle in a way I had never felt before.

Later, Michelle visually went to the edge of her garden and pictured a door there. She saw herself taking the door off the hinges, allowing heavenly beings direct access, and invited them in to visit her.

In my inner garden, I saw myself sitting by the lake and invited God to sit there beside me. Feeling that presence beside me was profound! It's one thing to go to the Buckingham Palace and see the queen of England stand on her balcony and wave, but can you imagine what it would feel like to have her come and sit with you in your garden content to just be in your presence? We felt the Divine presence from within—we felt accepted, loved unconditionally, humbled, renewed, and happy spending time with the Divine in our inner gardens.

To experience a spiritual connection in your life,
welcome Divine presence from within.

Feeling so much joy and connection in these experiences, we started asking some new questions. What is happening when we use mana gardening techniques? How is

130

it that we can access a level of wisdom and insight that we previously did not have conscious access to? Seeking to better understand this presence and positive energy led us to explore the basics of the consciousness in forming healthy spiritual connections.

Consciousness, as a field of study, is not fully scientifically understood, so the purpose of this discussion is for description only, and not scientific validation. With that said, let's clarify our use of some terms. The *conscious mind* is the active, thinking and planning mind, and it includes whatever you may be focused upon or perceiving at the moment: talking on the phone, cutting vegetables, music playing, feeling a pain in your back, organizing your desk, the birds chirping, the kids fighting, reading this book, riding your bike, or any ongoing thoughts.

The *subconscious mind* is like a security camera, aware of everything around us, but unlike a mechanical piece of recording equipment, it also takes in what is unseen. The subconscious mind not only records all the movements, conversations, and noises going on around us, but also notes what is consciously unnoticed—all of the nuances, subtleties, and unspoken feelings that seem to escape our day-to-day radar.

Subconsciously, all of these images, with their emotional and intuitive context, are actually caught, recorded, and saved forever. We were taught that the subconscious is a part of the mind that is not in focal awareness, but in that definition perhaps we fail to recognize that the subconscious mind is actually aware of everything going on around us.

We believe that by occupying the conscious, thinking, planning mind with the activity of imagining and visualizing ourselves relaxed in the sacred garden space, it thereby allows the information within the intuitive, reflective, subconscious mind a voice—an opportunity to be heard or sensed.

Stated another way, when you are mana gardening and distracting your conscious mind of thoughts by using the imagination, your conscious mind is placed into a passive, observational mode that may allow access to all the information stored within the subconscious mind, to a broader field of information. In this state, the conscious mind is passive, yet still aware. Mana gardening appears to allow the conscious and subconscious minds to meet, tune in to one another, and work together as a team, supporting you in being able to access and retrieve this valuable information, as insight or perhaps intuition.

Unfortunately, what we have been taught, and most everything we do, teaches us to let the active, thinking, planning mind rule our lives. We tend to give only the conscious mind an opportunity to drive, when the subconscious mind actually holds far more information and thus knows us better; in this habit of blocking out our subconscious mind, we lose sight of what we really want.

With mana gardening techniques, we can learn to let each part of the mind have some time to drive our lives.

Perhaps we can finally be happy, because we have a way to let the intuitive, reflective mind tell the active, thinking mind where we really want to go and what we really want to do.

In addition to having access to a broader field of information, we seem to be experiencing a spiritual higher power, the Divine, God, universal goodness, or universal consciousness. Feeling more in tune with the subtle energies of everything around us we believe that, while mana gardening, we are opening ourselves up to sensing this pervasive, forthright force. When allowing the conscious and subconscious minds to mingle and work together, and through being relaxed and open to higher states, we somehow relax further and open a door to the ultimate Divine wisdom that lies within us.

This state we reach or access is analogous to meditators entering a theta brainwave state, a highly creative state at 4-7 Hz brainwave cycles per second where those experiencing this state seem to touch the creative force. While mana gardening, you may witness and come into contact with your higher self, a higher power, God, the creative force, or universal goodness, and perhaps your soul.

This is the richest part of mana gardening for us! By simply inviting the energy of God, or the Divine to join us in our inner gardens we not only feel filled with love, joy, and wellbeing, this spiritual connection also creates balance, direction, and purpose in our lives.

We believe this power or guidance that we tap into is in fact of a Divine nature because the guidance we receive is always in our best interest and the best interest of all concerned. Many times, in consulting with the energy from within and following that guidance, we feel that without such consultation, we reflexively would not make such choices or even think of such choices on our own. We always feel the answers are better than what we personally could conceive of and must be coming from a higher perspective, which leads us to trust this guidance wholeheartedly.

Because we get answers that seem to resonate with our truest natures, and our deepest soul desires, we feel that this inner garden space allows us to tune into our hearts, perhaps our soul. We recognize what we truly want, what is best for us, and we somehow feel that the information or guidance we receive is right or true for us—leading us to feel *guided*. There is a forthright power from within, what the Hawaiians call mana. This Divine stream, our mana, flowing within us is a beautiful, humbling, and empowering experience.

Regarding the positive nature of our spiritual experiences, I was raised to believe there is good and there is evil. But I was also taught that evil has no hope—evil has actions that give grief, sorrow, anguish, or torment to another person—and that instructions from God, or Divine consciousness, don't do any of these.

We decided that, if these insights or experiences of what we believe are from a higher power ever show us any sign of hopelessness, despair, anguish, or torment, or if it ever asks anything of us that would bring even one ounce of this negativity to any other person, we would simply visualize taking this energy to the gates of our gardens and banishing it forever.

To this day, Michelle and I can both say that the experiences and insights we received from our gardens has been not only 100 percent positive, the only request of us has been to work at holding ourselves to being 100 percent positive, too! We believe this was and is possible because we follow a cardinal inner garden guideline always: *Never allow any negativity into your inner garden.* Stated another way: *Do not allow anything in your inner garden that may disturb the peace and sacredness of your personal heaven. Mana* essentially means power. And mana can be good or bad. Michelle's innocence brought God in. Having inner garden discernment (by allowing absolutely NO negativity in the garden) sealed the fact that we are only entertaining the forthright energy of good, healthy mana.

As an example of the garden encouraging positivity, we all have some difficult people in our lives; ones we love, but can't understand or maybe cannot find much compassion for; those we want to help, but don't know how to help; those whose reasons for self-destruction have always escaped us. Their needs comprise some impossibly long list that even if we could manage to get through it—it wouldn't really matter—more would just be added to those lists.

Before this spiritual connection was so prevalent for Michelle and me, we gave these folks lots of space to wallow in their misery. We believed that we were lessening their burdens by finding a way to fix their problems and joining them in criticizing those who made their lives harder (all of which caused us to feel negative emotion too).

With the Divine presence in our gardens, we clearly understand that we are not being asked to continue to "serve" others in this way. In fact, we find ourselves not being asked to do anything for our suffering friends and family other than provide a positive light in their presence and simply focus on all things good. In doing so, we no longer add to their burdens and provide positive energy for them instead, without adding negative energy to our own lives.

Another benefit of mana gardening with the energy of God or the Divine, is that it is clear that we are not being asked to work on anyone other than ourselves. The focus is never on the others, it is always on us, to be a positive light at all times, to be optimistic for their new job, happy for new relationships coming their way, and upbeat in every step we make with everyone around us, including ourselves.

A great example of this was when someone totally surprised Michelle with behavior she didn't expect. She and a friend had an important agreement that was in place for years (in writing I must add). They had both cooperated with the agreement, and because of this, everyone involved benefitted. Now, it was her friend's turn to uphold the agreement and there this person was backing out of it without any prior communication. Disappointment and disbelief were the feelings Michelle felt. She also felt a lack of integrity about this person. After a few moments of fuming (spinning out) she went into her inner garden and relaxed next to a beautiful waterfall. She then asked the wisdom within her garden, "How do I handle this?"

Interestingly, the garden showed her that she needed to focus on her own integrity—to be *pleased* with *herself* for upholding the agreement, for being integral, for following up what she believed was right, with her action. Actually, what she received from her garden was a healthy dose of self-love. She felt love and respect for herself and basked in that feeling for quite some time.

Then, from within her garden, she imagined all the negative energy she held surrounding the situation in real life leaving her body and being *absolutely unable* to affect her. Her garden went completely white for a moment and then went back to its brilliant scenic colors.

In this case, the inner garden showed Michelle that focusing on her friend's behavior, or any of the negative feelings she felt were neither useful nor valuable; that it would be wiser and more productive to use her energy to feel good about herself.

Until we felt this benevolent presence, Michelle and I didn't understand how important it is to simply be a light of hope and positivity for ourselves and others and not a bearer of burdens and negativity! (We also had no idea how hard it truly is to not be negative!)

With the energy of God, or Love, it became clear to us that we are never expected to take on anyone else's pain, suffering, or struggle, or to focus on anyone's ways of being that we disagree with; we are only expected not to add to it. This was a huge change for us both. It was 100 percent positive and yet it was not necessarily what we would have chosen with our old, negative patterns.

Have you ever heard the phrase, "The peace that surpasses all understanding?" Spiritually connected people understand that there is an incredible relief, an empowerment, and a joy from feeling the presence of God or a higher power in your life and knowing that you are only being asked to work on yourself.

We now understand that overwhelming joyous feeling of peace from within ourselves. With the essence of the Divine in our inner gardens, we see that there is always optimism for this person or that person, but there is never misplaced responsibility!

The more we welcome this benevolent presence, the more we work on being stronger in holding onto our positive energy, so that we can use it to energize others in positive ways.

One of my biggest spiritual miracle moments came when my husband found that he had tumors in his liver. They hospitalized him in a private room where he and I curled up together in the small bed and held each other. Throughout the night, I mana gardened many times with God; at times I saw myself with my head on his shoulder crying.

Surprisingly, when I would start to cry, I not only intuitively felt that I needed to stop crying, I also felt at peace and that my husband would grow old with me. Throughout that night, I felt Christ sitting with me, wrapping his arms around me, sharing his strength with me, and I was encouraged to be stronger, not only for myself, but also for my husband.

In one of my needy moments, I reached out to my very spiritual aunt, who told me to ask for a sign from God—a tangible sign that God was truly with me and that my husband really would be all right. She didn't entertain even a second of my despair; instead she offered me her strength and hope.

So I did. A rose popped into my head, so I asked God in my inner garden, to put a rose in the hospital room before sunrise as a sign that my husband was going to be ok. In Hawaii, we enjoy an abundance of tropical flowers, so roses are the last flower I would expect to see if anyone in our family brought flowers. I sat on the bed and lay my head on my husband's chest, and in the midst of my darkest moments, I was able to see myself enter my garden and lay my head on the shoulder of Christ and feel renewed strength that I could offer to my husband.

When I focused on being a light of positive energy, I could soothe my husband fearlessly and lovingly. As I closed my eyes, I pictured God and me on that terrace by the lake in the big easy chairs, and all was well. It was a comfort that words cannot describe.

Around five a.m., a nurse walked into the room and wrote *Rose* in big letters on the white board above my husband's bed, and said this was her name. I burst into tears of joy *knowing* that God had reached out into this world to give me strength and hope! The tumors turned out to be very slow growing and my husband and I live fearlessly even today, years later.

We don't focus on what could happen, or what the future may hold, instead we focus on what is great today! This strength appears not to come from the old me, because the old me knows how to worry myself sick. With this higher power in my life anytime I desire, I can hold onto my strength and work towards the only thing that is truly asked of me—being positive always.

This is a total transformation from how I lived my life even just a few years ago. I think back to my days before mana gardening, and, in this situation, I would have been destructively spinning out in worry, fear, and sorrow. Even with mana gardening, I had a few moments where I sought out others to pray with me. All I needed, though, was God beside me and he was there the moment I welcomed him in.

Due to my inner practice, I live happier, and because I spend time with this energy of oneness, or the Divine, it is easier to live my life empowered with positive energy, and joyful for everything! It has not been easy to stop those old judgmental and detrimental habits—it's often a reflex to have a negative opinion about something. But for Michelle and me now, it is our daily work to steer our thoughts and hold ourselves in a mindset of positivity.

What we feel through mana gardening is that we can reach this zen place where the creative force, the energy of God, is always present. This is where we allow our conscious and subconscious minds to commune when we are basking in our sacred space. If you want to walk a path with God, you have to walk the path God walks and be open to walking there with the energy of Love.

Many believe the only way to have faith is to participate in religion or be around religious people. Maybe we don't have to do this. Maybe all we need to do is let both parts of our mind spend some time together with an open door to God, or a higher presence. This seems to allow that stream of inner guidance, Divine energy, our mana, to flow, giving us faith—our own personal experiences with God.

Mana gardening provides us the opportunity of walking a spiritual pathway that needs no church, history, opinions, and/or experiences of others. Yet, when we feel inspired to go to a spiritual service, we go and feel the connection deeper than before.

Michelle's upbringing included a relationship with Jesus, so when Michelle feels it's needed she visualizes Jesus' arms wrapped around her. She is free to trade her worries, burdens, or fears for hope and strength. She is free to ask for guidance, energy, or clarity to balance her life even when it seems upside down or appears that all hope is lost. Always, she is reminded to work on herself, to know herself, and to stand strong in the zone of optimism.

We have come to believe that being spiritually connected has helped us build a stronger faith and a more innate sense of clarity than when we do our own thinking and let our conscious selves run our lives exclusively.

We invite you to try this for yourself. You can invite any energies or spiritual beings, who you would feel would nurture you, into your garden: Jesus, Buddha, angels, the energy of nature, Krishna, Divine Love, Creator Source, your own inner strength, unity, oneness…. The one guideline is that all of your reflections should center on a healthy you and what needs to change about you, for you to live happier.

By tapping into this stream of Divine wisdom that lives inside of you, you can learn to be that light of 100 percent positive energy for yourself and you will become that light for others!

MAKANA:

As you are mana gardening, create a door that leads directly to Divine consciousness or God.

Remove the door from the doorway and then speak out that all things in your highest and best interest are welcome in your inner world.

Welcome to the spiritual path.

CHAPTER 10

THE NO-SPIN POWER TOOL

While writing this book, my father struggled through a quadruple bypass, my younger brother lost his life to a crippling disease, and my husband suffered a stroke; these were only my personal struggles—professionally my life was just as complicated. In a time when my life was completely upside down, mana gardening gave me the skills I needed to change my perspective and thus change my life. I remained strong, was surprisingly happy, felt loved, and gave love lavishly to those I cared about.

I learned to recognize and stop myself at the slightest hint of an emotional spin. My days were filled with courage rather than despair. I often wonder where I would be right now if I had only my old ways of coping. Mana gardening had become my priceless life-affirming process. I was able to live and thrive, not simply survive!

One night, Michelle and I went to a candle-lit service of only music and prayer. In my old ways, I would have been lost in my fears. There, in the candlelight, I felt connected to everyone in my life, and so very strong. Tears of joy ran down my face without my feeling sad. My life was upside down, and in spite of all the trials and troubles that came my way, I felt strong and *my worry bank was empty*! I was free from the life I lived before, and for the first time ever, I said, "Thank you," to my garden. It was as if I could hear every part of my heart and soul answering back, "You're welcome!"

Just then, Michelle placed her hand on my back, and I felt her strength too, and we both smiled. Life wasn't easy for either of us, but we were empowered rather than weak.

Michelle was confronting her own uphill struggle. She faced divorce from a man she loved very much and was about to move her children thousands of miles away. They would be closer to family and her children would remain close to both parents. Although this move was what she wanted, she knew she would have to start her life all over again on her own. In leaving a very good job, she now faced a financial struggle as well as an emotional one. She too, stood on a rocky road, and yet we were both simply happy. It was then I knew, without any doubt, that we discovered for ourselves a very simple way to live better, and that path to sustained happiness came from learning to live in the garden within.

That night, I felt inspired to make a list of the greatest tools we received from mana gardening. It taught us a way to instantly feel relaxed, peaceful and happy which made us healthier. The joy of a spiritual connection kept us feeling connected to ourselves and God. Feeling insightful toward others as well as ourselves has shown us the paths we want for our lives. Above all, every day is easier, because going within taught us to live spin-free! In making this list and prioritizing it, learning to live spin-free is the most powerful everyday tool for living better.

Before mana gardening, whenever I found myself feeling hurt, I allowed my thinking mind to go round and round into a negative emotional spin, without any idea what was really wrong. I am sad to say, in the past, I fell into this trap with everyone I ever loved. Sadly, these moments of spinning out would go on and on without any defined outcome, hurting everyone. Worst of all, I had no idea what I really wanted or how to fix it. The more Michelle and I used mana gardening, the easier it became to recognize how detrimental this habit was to our happiness.

Recognizing the start of the spin and stopping ourselves from going there saved us from so much self-inflicted, emotional pain. Spinning out emotionally is a bad choice; it is a time-wasting, negative-energy-perpetuating bad habit. Allowing your thinking mind to spin out emotionally can ruin your life. It is a pattern that robs you of every chance you have to be happy in the moments at hand.

To be happy, you have to be able to recognize the beginning of a spin, and instead of feeding the spin, place yourself in your inner garden. You relax and then focus all that wasteful spin energy into reducing all the thoughts in your head into one brief sentence that states what is wrong or what it is you want. Spinning out emotionally is just stacking un-serving thoughts up in a worry bank and letting them take over your life.

Michelle and I developed something we call the *no-spin power tool*. It is a simple system to break this bad habit that we recognized as a major stumbling block to maintaining daily happiness. Best of all, this tool has reduced all of our struggles to one-sentence concepts instead of long-winded conversations that could be rehashed over and over again for months and months.

Living in the garden and using this no-spin power tool made it easier to get to those "aha" moments where Michelle and I uncovered exactly what was wrong and exactly what we really wanted or needed. What we never understood before mana gardening is that you can't possibly work out anything in the real world unless you have worked it out first with your inner self and know how you feel or what you really want!

So, let's first think of relationships without the no-spin power tool. Remember those long, drawn-out "we need to talk" moments? Those "talks" never fixed anything. They only made our lives harder and our loved ones miserable. In truth, we did not know what we really wanted at all, but we would go round and round with our loved ones, leaving everyone exhausted.

When Michelle and I stopped spinning out, relating to other people became easier. The good news is that you never have to take anyone else or yourself down this pathway ever again. If you want to live better each and every day, then try the no-spin power tool for yourself.

The first step is to recognize when your mind is spinning and stop it immediately.

Step 1: Recognize when you are beginning to spin out. When you feel upset, frustrated, or unhappy with yourself, another person, or a situation, immediately stop the spinning thoughts by placing yourself into your inner garden to relax mentally. Feel the feelings, but do not feed the feelings with additional negative or unbeneficial thoughts. Just relax from within your gar-

den. Take in the scenery and the peace. Allow any negative feelings to dissipate.

Once you feel your body relax, use that moment of relaxation to ask yourself, "What is wrong?" or "What do I want?" depending on the situation. Listen for the answer, and intend to focus it in one concise 5-10 word sentence. The relaxed zone of the garden allows you to access your own inner wisdom, which is excellent at stating what really is wrong, or what you want, in the simplest terms, without emotion.

Here is an example: your dear friend is 15 minutes late, again, which is going to make you late for a very important dinner date. You feel yourself, as the minutes tick by, welling up with frustration, anger and many other emotions. Instead of feeding all of that with negative thought upon negative thought and blowing up when your friend finally arrives, you recognize that you are beginning to spin out and decide to close your eyes and go within. You enter your sacred inner garden and feel some of those emotions as they start to subside. Once you feel yourself relax into your nurturing space you ask, "What is wrong here?" You listen and learn how you really feel. You then communicate to your dear friend upon her arrival with a short, simple, honest statement, "You are 15 minutes late again and I have a very busy schedule and feel disrespected when you continually arrive late."

150

How refreshing would it feel if you chose to know yourself, chose not to spin out, and chose to express your true feelings in a way that was respectful of yourself and your friend?

So, while those around you may not do this, it is now possible for *you* to do this. *You could be the person in your world that refuses to spin. You could know and express yourself this well.*

The bonus is that we all learn by living, and if you choose to live this way, those you love may learn to live this way, too. Wouldn't it be refreshing if communication were this direct and honest? When you stop giving in to the bad habit I like to call *milking the spin,* you can truly have honest, loving relationships and you can avoid the arguing or poor communication that leads to resentment, negativity, and even failure in some of the very best of relationships.

For some cases you will want to use step 2. For example, when you want to request a change in behaviour or request what you desire from others. In step 2, you will need to determine what it will take to actually have what you truly want. While relaxing in your inner garden, intend to organize your thoughts into a very simple, reasonable, one-sentence request that is easy for anyone to accomplish. The key is that the request must be achievable.

Let's say you honestly forgot to pick up the dry cleaning after your spouse reminded you five times. You arrive home in your forgetful zone, facing their disappointment and frustration, asking, "What's wrong?" You have no idea what the problem is, but you know where this conversation is going; you are about to head down that nasty road where you both spin a million circles. Your spouse is upset, angry, and frustrated, and you have no clue what is *really* going on. Ugly words spill back and forth needlessly, and for what? A few pieces of laundry?

Every one of us has been there, and some of us live there consistently. It's painful and accomplishes nothing. In the end, you find yourself in the midst of an ugly fight that you knew was coming the moment you sincerely cared enough to ask, "What's wrong?" Even worse, you saw it all falling apart before it started happening; you could feel it before you even asked. You just played spin-out with someone you love, an exhausting and cruel game in which everybody loses.

What if you asked, "What's wrong?" and your loved one replied with one simple, achievable response, "You forgot to stop at the cleaner's, and it hurts when you forget the things I need. Will you please go back out and grab them?" They then move on asking you about your day. Can you imagine what life would be like if your loved one saw you coming in the door empty-handed, knew what they wanted or needed, refused to spin out about it, and chose to express themselves concisely?

If you can't identify what it takes to have what you want without an endless list of demands to correct the problem, then you can't expect your problems to ever be fixed. Again, it is all about knowing yourself and making your choices from within before trying to work out anything in person with anybody else. When allowing yourself to spin out, and demanding a long list of requirements for resolution, you hijack your happiness and hold yourself, and those who love you, hostage.

> *Step 2: Ask yourself, in the peacefulness of your inner garden, what it will take to fix whatever is wrong. Intend to condense the action you need into one easy-to-achieve, concise sentence being willing to give instant appreciation and complete forgiveness when it's done.*

At first, I had a hard time with step 2. Most of the time, I really, truly could not find an achievable answer. Often, I would ask for an apology, but I didn't really want an apology. If my loved one said they were sorry, I could not put it down and say it's fixed—I'd still be mad. This problem wasn't theirs, it was my inability to know what it would take to forgive and truly feel happy again.

If the answer to a problem isn't an apology, then I cannot ask for an apology. If I want never to be forgotten, as in the dry cleaning example, then my demands are not humanly possible. If I ask for a change in behavior, then it has to be easy to achieve and I have to be able to give instant appreciation and complete forgiveness when it's done. This is the hardest part for me.

I can easily claim what's wrong (Step 1). However, when I can't state a simple way to fix it, what do I do? I seem to want more than what is really possible from others to correct the situation (Step 2). I honestly can't accept just an apology; it's just not that easy for me. I often lock myself out at step 2.

I had to face the truth about myself and learn step 3. I had to learn how to let go, because what I needed from others to make things right was usually not even possible for them to do. The truth is that no one could ever make me happy until I learned to make simple and achievable requests.

My problem at step 2 usually had nothing to do with being forgotten or feeling hurt; it had to do with the realization that I like to aim my spinning out at others, and that is not fair. I not only had to learn to stop my own spin, but I also had to stop spinning out on other people, blaming them, and reviving that spin because I could not let go of what that hurt or offended me.

Being unable to let go was the essence of my real problem. I had to learn that when I chose to accept an apology from someone, I then had a responsibility to treat him or her as if nothing bad ever happened.

Step 3: Let go of it all—not just the spinning out and the hurt, but also the judgment, the blame, the punishment, the debate, the problem, the need for resolution—let go of everything that has even an ounce of negativity in it, and also let go of the potential solution and any outcome. In fact, if you want to continue to love this person you may have to let go of it all without any resolution whatsoever.

It seems so easy to say, but it is not easy at all. Letting go is actually the hardest part of the whole process, but it is one of the most vital aspects about being happy that living in the garden has taught me. Not only for myself, but also for those I love and care about, I had to learn how to simply state what is wrong, and, if possible, ask the other person to fix it, but most of all, I had to learn to let go of my hurt and disappointment. With mana gardening, I came to realize it was time I loved my spouse, children, and close friends more than my desire to be right or have all my needs met.

In the briefest sense, the no-spin power tool can be used for any situation and consists of these three simple steps:

Step 1: Know what is wrong or what you want in one sentence, or let it all go.

Step 2: Know what you want to fix the problem in one sentence, or let it all go.

Step 3: Let go of both Steps 1 and 2 and any outcome that you desire, *completely*.

Learning to let go doesn't mean ignoring repetitive habits or hurtful behaviors of others. With repetitive behaviors that are harmless to everyone, you can just float downstream and let those behaviors go so that you and your loved one can be happy together. But repetitive behaviors that are hurtful or painful to anyone involved, that occur with someone you care about, need to be voiced and addressed.

In these situations, reach for the no-spin power tool to determine what you want and offer the person a concise solution. If the behavior doesn't change, then you might need to avoid this person, situation, or place altogether and/or seek professional assistance. The no-spin power tool can help make a large problem smaller, more manageable, and fixable.

The clear-mindedness of halting your own spinning will also help you recognize when you are being drawn into the spin of others. This self-awareness will boost your confidence to say, "So long," to those who take far more of your time and energy than you are willing to give. Recognizing when other people are making your life harder is a very important life skill, one we often downplay to our own detriment.

Living spin-free puts you on the road to being truly
healthy and happy
in all of your relationships.

With the no-spin power tool I love more honestly and my loved ones are safer with me. For the first time in his life with me my husband is truly safe in asking me what to do when I am needy. He can now be confident that I won't take him into the spin or punish him, by making him jump through a never-ending set of invisible hoops to win my happiness. I now have solutions that are achievable. My hubby is still a bit bullish and ever so unyielding sometimes, but when I let go, there isn't anything to fight over. He hasn't embraced the no-spin power tool as Michelle and I have, but he has learned to disagree "cleaner," and thus we spin less, primarily because I stopped doing it.

When I see him spinning out, I ask him to tell me what exactly is wrong, and then tell me in one sentence what he really needs me to do to make things right. I can help him focus, and I don't take his non-focus personally—he really has no idea what he wants. I now know that anyone with a long list of needs hasn't taken the time to figure out what they really want. I deflect their lists by asking them to take some time to themselves to consider the one thing they need the most.

When I know what I need from my husband and love him with or without it, I am easier to love, and he is free to be himself. This is where I am living these days, and it's beginning to pour into everything else. There is less and less of a need to even ask for that one-sentence correction, because he has started finding it on his own.

In fact, I cringe when I hear anyone say, "We need to talk," because most of the time it really means that they have no idea what they want. The saddest part is that everyone involved is going to suffer the face-to-face negative escalation that accompanies most efforts to "talk" about it. I have started to teach my older children that when people say, "We need to talk," they should ask that person to explain in two short sentences, what is wrong and how to fix it!

With mana gardening, our lives are about clarity, and with the no-spin power tool our actions are based on having already discovered what we really want and knowing how to have it!

MAKANA:

Practice identifying moments when you are spinning out emotionally—those times when your thoughts are racing through fears or judgments and you feel stress. Use the no-spin power tool to stop spinning and count how many times you stop yourself from spinning out.

Every time you catch yourself leaning towards a negative spiral, and stop it, it is worth 10 dollars.

For the next three days, keep track of how many emotional dollars you add to your life each day and notice if you feel happier and more well-balanced.

CHAPTER 11

THE ANSWERS LIE WITHIN

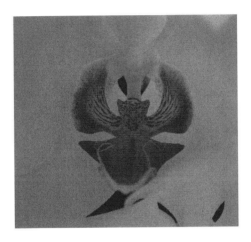

Through mana gardening, Michelle and I stumbled onto something profound: a way inward. By going within, we began to know clearly what we wanted in our lives, and thus our starting point for everything shifted. When Michelle and I light gardened together (a collaborative process described in chapter 6), we simultaneously experienced an effortless intuitive flow and ease. This reminded us of something that, as cell biologists, we have witnessed repeatedly, that we cannot dismiss—one of the most simple and exciting truths of cellular behavior.

These tiny blobs called cells, which have no brain or emotions, have some innate behaviors that go beyond reflexes. If you drop a single cell into one side of a Petri dish, and another cell into the opposite side, you can predict their behavior. First they will pause, displaying limited activity. It appears that not much is happening as the cell is not reproducing; yet, on the inside, the cells are quite active metabolically. (I like to think they are reflecting inward, taking stock in their wellbeing, making repairs and assuring they are viable and ready to do what they were intended to do.) Then they will signal by releasing chemicals in an effort to "call out" to see if there are other cells close by.

If other cells nearby have similar functions or compatible needs, they will recognize those signals, mobilize, and reach toward each other, getting closer until they touch. They then focus on replication and serving their purpose by working together with the neighboring cells, including the new cells they are creating around them.

Throughout this intermingling of signals, stretch to touch, and dance of replication, they do only what they were created to do: find others like themselves, serve their purpose, and avoid harm—mindlessly, some may say. A cell has no brain, no memories, and no issues; it is the most basic form of life, and yet in its simplicity of behaviors it is perhaps the most brilliant. Within us lie these genius cellular building blocks that are simply better at living than we are.

I am a mother to many children and yet I am not sure that I have taught my children these simple and vital basic skills already known within us by each and every cell in our body: to know their purpose, to seek like-minded souls, and to avoid harm.

I spent decades guiding my children to get along with others, play nicely, and work in groups. But without a solid idea of themselves, how can they begin to seek out and draw closer to those who share similar life goals, or recognize those who would help or even harm them?

Can you imagine if we all possessed these simple life skills? Most of us do not. The truth is, we were never given permission or taught how to look inward, to know ourselves, and to look at our own wants and desires—if you know the attributes of what you want, then you can recognize them in others.

Instead, to our own detriment, we were taught to look outward, as if knowing yourself was self-centered. Enlightened souls, like Gandhi, Christ, and Buddha, suggested that we start from within, but our society doesn't quite teach us how to do this. In fact, we have likely been taught *not* to do this, and as such we are missing a very simple connection to our own happiness.

If you don't know what you want from life, your happiness is and always will be at the mercy of everyone around you. With mana gardening, knowing what you want isn't selfish at all: it is fundamental to being happy, and when you are happy, you affect the world in positive ways.

When great teachers say look inward, they do not mean in a self-centered way, but in a positive, self-reflective way. Michelle and I felt challenged to change our base perspective from *act and react* to *reflect and move forward*. Our minds were filled with new ideas! We were excited that changing our starting point from looking outward to reflecting inward first did not require dismantling anything about ourselves; it simply required adding some fresh new ideas to how we approached things.

I wanted my children to experience this independence, this self-awareness, this simple clear-mindedness that can lead to personal happiness. So, with my twins, I decided to try some of these new techniques to get them to begin to focus inward.

For example, like many times before, there was an argument over their desire for the same toy. Normally I would give the toy to one for a set amount of time and then give the toy to the other for an equal amount of time.

This time I took the toy away. I made the twins sit down, pause, reflect, think, and consider all the toys in the toy box. Then I let them go over to the toy box to pull out only one toy, but I told them if they chose the same thing, they had to sit down and we would start all over again.

They reached in and pulled out their own choices, and then I sent them in different directions to play on their own for a while. It was 30 minutes of absolute peace and quiet, plus they were both happy! My hope is that by practicing taking time out to reflect inward, it will become a habit not to focus on what they didn't get, but refocus on what other choices they have.

What if children were taught to look at a problem by themselves and then identify a solution they could accomplish on their own? In the school classroom the focus is usually on teaching kids how to work with others, yet, unless taught to know themselves first, how can they ever work effectively with anyone else?

We push them to compete and excel without giving them the time they need to even know what really makes them happy. Report cards rate a child on how well they work with others, and rate how well they work independently too, but how can they really work independently if everyone is doing the same project and everyone will be graded in comparison to one another? To work independently, there has to be a complete sense of safety in oneself.

What if there was an aspect to my children's classroom education that allowed them to work solely on their own, without ever having to display their work to anyone other than the teacher and they had the safety net that the teacher would never rate their individual efforts? What if the teacher would simply ask my child, "What do you want from this, and what would you need to feel truly happy with what you have done?" without being critiqued? I don't want to complain about our education here, because we as parents have more opportunity to teach our children than anyone else. What I am saying is that, if we shift our focus a small bit, we may be able to help our children become happier people.

In addition to looking for ways to help my twins change their focus from outward to inward, I also began to look for ways to help them recognize an emotional spin, and stop it. I began to wonder… when I am listening to or letting them vent, am I really helping them, or am I training them to hold themselves hostage to their own anxiety? Then I experienced a moment of realization: that sometimes I don't need to try to fix anything for my children, and in fact, maybe I am not helping at all even by listening.

It started with a child in a tirade. I could have gone into my parenting lecture about how it won't matter one day, but instead I just hugged my son. He let go in a relaxed way, right away, which made me feel the drama was just that— drama. I simply said, "I love you. Now take some time to think about what you want to do," and then he walked away. I gave his spin no extra voice and he had a skip in his step!

Michelle and I understand the art of the hug; we know to hug our children and allow them to let go of us first. If they hug and go quickly, they are less needy. If they hold on, they may be hurting and need more attention. Paying attention to a hug tells us so much. When it's a serious issue or a child lingers in the hug we listen more attentively, are more responsive, and give the child more kindness and compassion.

Michelle and I use this measuring stick all the time—it allows us to know where our children are emotionally. It is a balancing act however; we want to nurture their needs, and we also want to teach *them* to nurture their own needs while not enabling them to milk their own spin and dig themselves deeper into negative emotion.

With the new me, when it's no big deal, I don't add to my children's issues; I simply remind them to choose for themselves what they want to do next, and go do it. I believe that this makes them actively responsible for their own happiness, and will hopefully teach them to begin to recognize when they are beginning to spin and to deflect it.

If we can offer our children anything from mana gardening, it is to teach them that true happiness is self-given and self-driven. What if we could empower our children with the tools necessary to know what path they want to take, to pull away from harmful situations, and to draw close to others with similar talents, values, or passions? We realized we had to teach them to see the world as a huge center of freedom, a buffet for them to experience and savor, and decide for themselves what they want to experience.

Your happiness is based solely on you and you must look inward
and decide on your own what that picture will be.

167

The direction of our parenting had to change—and this is the paradigm shift—from *fostering looking outward* to *encouraging starting from within.* From an outward focus to an inward focus, we have to teach children to be happy on their own and know what they want, and we have to teach them that this is just as important as working with others.

Not to dilute or discount the importance of group dynamics, but why do we reach for that first? We, as a society, place far too much emphasis in team efforts, playgroups, and the like without making sure our children stand strong, solid, and confident in who they are on their own. An outward focus is asking what does everyone else do, what do they wear, how do they look, how do they act, and determining your happiness based on those answers.

Michelle and I are aware that it is valuable for kids to have some time alone, inwardly focused, considering themselves and what makes them happy, so that their perspective of themselves is based on knowing themselves. We knew we needed to teach our children to be and feel happy based on their own actions without building their idea of happiness based on how others perceive them.

Interestingly, we found that confidence is a beneficial by-product when you focus inward and know yourself and what you want. A confident person is less shaken by the opinions of others and less needy for approval. For example, if I call you a stupid person, you may feel bad.

If you're a blonde, and I call you a stupid brunette, you would laugh, because the insult doesn't match who you are. A confident person is more likely to be emotionally unaffected and regard such insults as missing the mark, without even taking in what was said, because the negative imagery doesn't match who they know themselves to be. Everything we were taught before forces us to look outward for validation, however, when you look outward for validation, self-confidence gets sabotaged and self-doubt becomes prevalent.

During the years leading up to their divorce, when Michelle looked outward toward her then-husband for validation, she got more doubt and less confidence; the more Michelle tried to work with her husband on his terms (the more she focused on him and his needs instead of focusing on herself and her needs), the more she felt rejected and flawed. She was focusing herself outward and letting him reflect back her worth and her value. This put her in a position where her self-esteem relied upon how he responded to her. Living outward allows us to feel rejected, denied, and dismantled by another, and it may not be intentional or even personal.

When she started looking inward, she got more confidence and less doubt. Her inner voice was heard by the most important person of all: Michelle herself. She liked whom she saw on the inside and refused to get caught up in the spin that would create a negative environment for her children.

An inward focus made her remain honest with herself and helped her be true to her heart, and she came to understand that her then-husband's negativity toward her was really his and had little to do with her. Michelle learned not to doubt herself, to deflect the negativity, and surround herself with people who valued her. This gave her more confidence and greater self-esteem.

Today, our starting point is always within, and because of this everything around us is changing for the better. Mana gardening enables us to live more like the cells in our bodies: it teaches us an easy way to simply take the time to remind us of what we want (which is our purpose), and to know who we trust so we seek kindred hearts. It also provides us a way to recognize and avoid less-than-favorable, or in some cases, harmful people and situations. It seemed to Michelle and me that the answer to everything lies within, and with this new starting point, the possibilities are endless.

MAKANA:

Stop right now and begin mana gardening. Feel yourself sink in and ask yourself what you want from your life for the next hour?

Ask yourself what, within reach, do you want from your day?

Visualize these occurring for you and feel your satisfaction from within your inner garden paradise.

This is creative mana gardening: what you focus on may appear in your real life.

Make sure you play with this every day!

CHAPTER 12

ATOP THE HIGHEST MOUNTAIN

Thinking we would finish this book before Michelle left for Peru, Michelle was on her flight before we got to this final chapter. We intended to complete it during her downtime from visiting sacred sites. Interestingly, I was going through my desk and found an ending chapter I had written over a year earlier. So, while she ascended the highest peaks, I sat down and reread this concluding chapter:

> Michelle and I have been practicing mana gardening for several years. Life is markedly sweeter just knowing that...

There is a simple way to tap into lifelong inner strength and happiness.

Even though we practice more and more, as we make it our habit, our reflex, the real world does creep in when we least expect it, and, each time, we must remind ourselves that...

True happiness is independent of everything and everyone around you.

Today, I found myself wrapped up in drama and stress surrounding my current home life with two teenagers in the house. I was actually washing dishes, when I visually plopped myself down on that big, white chair overlooking the lake in my garden and sighed a big sigh of decompression. My husband took notice of the change in my stance, and my faraway gaze—the act of mana gardening changed my posture and everything about my presence—away from the stressed and back to the relaxed.

"Where did you just go right now?" he asked.

"Far away," I said and smiled, but I was not even looking at him.

"But you're still there," he said.

I had to smile. I have come to the place where I can be in the garden in my mind and still carry on a conversation in real life. Even more interesting was the fact that, emotionally, I remained in that big, soft, garden chair and his interruptions did not distract me from my much-needed relaxation.

Even more exciting was the fact that I didn't feel the need to leave my inner garden and yet continued to talk to him. Thus, both places, the feeling of being here and now plus the land far, far away, were mine simultaneously, and, with this, my entire moment was markedly better.

"Teenagers," my husband said, rolling his eyes; he too was feeling tired of the drama. Now, I should say that he and I had already survived many teenagers, and what we were living now with these two boys wasn't nearly as complicated as what we had endured with some of the older kids. Still, it was needless stuff that simply wastes everyone's time and drains all the positive energy.

Yes, I am tired, too, I thought, but the me in my inner garden wasn't exhausted and wasn't worn out, which allowed me to say out loud, "My teenagers." And rather than saying it with disdain, I said it out loud lovingly.

In saying it this way, I noticed myself feeling upbeat, loving, and loved. I no longer felt like, *oh gosh those kids,* but rather my attitude was now turned around—my perspective had changed on its own—by just being in the garden mentally.

The only thing in life we truly have the power to change is our perspective.

I felt a rush of joy, for my attitude had almost effortlessly turned around. My automated better perspective was now changing my emotional self for the better, and it was happening on its own! My better perspective had turned my husband around too, and he smiled back at me happily.

He laughed. "Wow, you really deserve their respect just for the way you feel lovingly about them, because they have been a handful lately." The truth was that my heart was no longer focused on their difficult ways; I simply saw my love for them most of all.

Mana gardening made it easier for me to decompress and get back to the real me, time and time again. But just now, I had let go of the worn-out, tired me. I felt clear-minded about my teenage sons with just a few seconds in my garden. I did nothing more than practice this:

Visualize your idea of paradise and allow yourself to be there.

I smiled at my husband and gave him a kiss on the cheek. "I would like to take some time off from being me. I am going to a bookstore to walk around and not talk to anyone; would that be okay?" He not only helped me sneak out the door without any kids, but also reminded me to turn off my phone.

My husband and I live on Oahu in a large farmhouse, and between us we are mom and dad to 15 children, many grown with children of their own. We have two teenagers and young twins at home, grandkids who visit, and older kids, parents, and dear friends who come to stay with us in Hawaii, so I rarely find time to myself, which isn't a large problem for me truly, because I rarely feel the need for it. Quite frankly, if I have car keys in hand, there is *always* someone asking to go with me.

For 99 percent of my life I love this, and I don't really suffer any because of it. For me, it is normal. There is no complaining in saying this now; I am looking at my life and simply acknowledging the fact that I am always busy, and that's okay for me. So to realize right then that I needed time to myself was a huge shift for me internally.

My husband surfs or swims almost daily, so he gets one to three hours per day free from everything; as such, he understood completely what I was asking for and was happy that I was actually taking time to myself.

I decided, in the bookstore, I would not speak to anyone and have no iPod either, just quiet. Yes, I would do some mana gardening, but I would also keep my body engaged in walking around and my eyes busy in glancing across book covers. So there I was at a nearby bookstore, "mana walking" for almost two hours.

Most of this time, my mind was looking out over the lake in my inner garden, but from time to time I reflected on my children and felt from within that all is well. Yes, all is well for most of the adult kids, and the few that were struggling had made their own poor choices. I felt confident from within that those with issues *needed* to struggle and not be rescued, so they could wise up.

The twins were fine, and the two teenagers were now facing that in-between time when you want to be an adult, but have only the experiences of a child. I didn't want to be mad at them for doing foolish kid stuff, or even for being disrespectful to me, but I couldn't permit them to behave this way either, stuck in donkey mode.

Within my garden, I realized that they were all right, and that I just needed to stay on track as a parent. So, I came to terms with myself: stay on track, don't get caught up in it, just do what a good parent does, keep holding the line, the rest is up to them.

I felt clear-minded about how normal it is for young people to think they have all the answers and not understand that the choices they make today could rob them of every chance they have to reach their own goals. I saw this all in my head now without exhaustion or negativity. I now felt only relief and love.

Because of this perspective change, I no longer felt the weight of the work it will take to once again pass through the teenage years; instead, I felt bathed in the love I have for them. Taking time to enjoy this relaxing clarity, I was reminded that...

Mana Gardening reveals how you perceive the people in
your life and identifies
the depth in which you value and trust them.

Then, as I was looking inward, I felt the need
to ask them right there in my head, in my inner
garden, "What is the one thing that I can do for
you to help you, and all of us really, when I get
irritated or mad at you?" I didn't feel an answer.
Instead, I felt, without a doubt, that this was the
question I needed to ask my sons face-to-face,
and I did so later that day.

In starting this conversation with them, I
told them that I felt they were fine, destined
to be great individuals when they grew up, yet
they were being rude, and that it was stuff that
should be easy for them to change. I followed
what I learned in mana gardening—focus and
keep it concise—which I am still learning day by
day to do.

I asked them to tell me one thing, and one
thing only, that they would want me to do for
them in regard to this problem; I was surprised
not only by their answers but that they knew
what they wanted. They are young, and yet
they seem to be better at knowing what they
want than I do. I wonder if, when we are young,

perhaps, we inherently know what we want, and as we get older, the life lessons make it harder for us to know what we really want.

Knowing what you want allows you to make things better in your life.

Either way, I knew that this moment, when we were open and talking, that they were both in and this alone made anything possible!

To love and be loved in a relationship, each person must be *in* and willing to let each other in, always.

For one of my sons, it was not what I could do, but what he wanted me not to do. He wanted me not to get angry and I agreed to try. He was honest about his part and what he should do to change it. He walked away from me feeling upbeat and positive.

The other son, too, had a simple request: "When you are really mad at me, can you give me 30 minutes to go sit outside and cool off so I don't say or do something more stupid?" This is hard for me; it's sort of being asked to let go while I am mad, but it's what he needed. My life with them began to change for the better. I felt myself relaxed and more at ease over their teenage days.

I mentally started bringing my teenagers into my inner garden to ask them what they wanted in an effort to meet their needs and I began to be more intuitive about them. I not only knew more often when things were off with them personally, but I also knew when they were beginning to go in the wrong direction.

I caught them both over and over again in the first steps of making poor choices. It was as if once they knew I had opened up my thoughts to them, they were opening up their thoughts to reveal to me what they themselves were uncertain about.

Mana Gardening can only show to others what you truly feel ready to reveal.

I wondered if these two young men of mine were hoping, from deep within, that I would catch on to the signals they were sending out, as if perhaps they were looking for direction, correction, and guidance without asking for it. They actually even seemed more at ease whenever they were caught in their antics. Sure, sometimes they would push me away or blow up with anger or emotion, but very quickly they were open and willing to talk, as if they too felt some relief that I was paying more attention to their unspoken signals.

So, back to my mana walk through the bookstore and my time out for good behavior. There I was in my garden, sitting in my big, soft, white chair overlooking the lake, and in reality standing in the art section of a bookstore, so my reality moment while mana gardening was filled with my favorite works of art. Life was upside down in my home, I let go of it all, and I felt wonderful.

Whenever the chaos of life is pushing your buttons...

float downstream...

and let it all go.

I managed to truly let it all go without forcing myself; the perspective change transformed my exhaustion to relief and love. With letting go, my relief was now being transformed into feelings of lightheartedness and, in some ways, even joy.

A few days later, I could not remember what I was mad about with my sons. In fact, when my mother brought up their rude behavior of the week before, I was actually caught off guard by her statements, and I really did not remember exactly what had happened.

With my teenagers, not only had I changed my perspective about what had happened and let go of how I felt about it all, I also chose to remember the positive and productive conversations we shared when I asked them what I could do to make it easier for us all to live together. I chose to focus my memories on the positive moments, and in doing so, I felt better, and so did they.

You can erase and replace unbeneficial memories
to strengthen yourself
emotionally and physically.

This forgetting the negative made me realize that the healthy patterns I became aware of had become my habit; only the love I felt remained. Before mana gardening, I dwelled upon this type of drama with my sons, allowing it to take control of my life and drain me of all of my energy.

184

The joy within me was contagious, and everything changed in how we all felt and interacted with each other. Our day-to-day lives were easier even though the teenagers still behaved, for the most part, like teenagers. There was no sorrow for the hard parts of our days, no anger locked up in my heart, no drama filling my head. There once again, at my kitchen window, I entered my inner garden, and as I glanced back to my lake, I visualized my husband walking toward me. I smiled at him, and he smiled back at me. *I want to love you more joyously*, I said in my head. *I want to love my family more joyously.*

Well, how do you plan to do that? I felt him say.

Without hesitation, this is what came from my heart: *I plan to live like Drew Barrymore in "50 First Dates". The dear girl had a head injury that made it impossible for her to remember anything from the day before, which gave her the freedom to live each day to the fullest! Simply because she had let go of everything, she had the freedom to fall in love all over again every single day of her life.* To let go was to live! I made a plan to try to actively let go of the day before and *live* each day more joyously!

In my garden stood my husband and I saw myself standing up to greet him as if I had not seen him in so very long. I held him close, breathed him in, and hugged him happily, and I knew that this is what it would take. To live and love each day more joyously, one has to meet and greet each person important in your life with a loving embrace and joy in your heart, and without any part of the past lingering around to take away from the present.

So, I took out my sword and visualized myself cutting the rope that hung from the sky tethered to my chair called yesterday, and then I cut the rope called disappointment. They fell to the ground, and I was free from them! There was joy in my step, and my heart felt light and carefree.

Later that day, I gave my 16-year-old a pat on the back, and the 13-year-old a hug. I sat down by my hubby and put my head on his shoulder and smiled at him; he hugged me and said, "Wow, that felt great!" It was simple—I was back to the center of mana gardening—all we can really change is our perspective, and mine was going to choose to live and love more joyously. The next day when I felt irritated at my hubby for something he forgot to do, I let it go and smiled at him instead. I was free from the ropes that had tied me to being unhappy. I never knew a head injury could feel so good!

When I read the above part of this last chapter, the part written over a year earlier, I felt tears of joy, because, long before he had his first stroke, I made a decision to try to always let go of what I perceived as my husband's errors. I had no idea, back when I first experienced this feeling, how very important this lesson would be, or that it would become, in many ways, the most important tool for holding on to everything beautiful about our marriage. In reading this year-old final chapter, I felt overcome with thankfulness to God for sparing my husband's life and for helping me see clearly what mana gardening has done for me in my own life.

It was there, in the garden, where Michelle and I came to understand that...

To experience a spiritual connection in your life, welcome Divine presence from within.

This spiritual connection offers me so much comfort when life hurts. This connection continues to grow stronger within me, and the joy I felt back when I wrote the year-old chapter, I feel even stronger today—and not just joy—I feel full of thankfulness for every part of my life.

Thankfulness is spiritual and a thankful heart is a happy heart, so when I am seriously struggling to change my perspective, I float downstream, figure out what I really want, and I reach for that spiritual connection by finding something for which to say thank you... my children, my life, my loving husband.

I not only feel closer to my family and myself, but also I feel oh so much closer to the Divine. It is a year later, and those teenagers who were driving us crazy last year are both on a better track today, and my habit of going within to know myself better has made all of this possible. So as I came to the last words of this final chapter, written over a year ago, I was once again in awe, because here was written:

> Keep mana gardening until it becomes the natural way you approach everything, every moment of your life, and put this final chapter away for now, because the final ending part hasn't happened yet.

I felt bathed in gratitude, in joy. I was excited from the bottom of my heart, because that was so true; at the time of the writing of the year-old chapter, we had not yet experienced what is in the previous three chapters. I sat there feeling a rush of all-encompassing contentment and connection.

Atop the mountain peaks of Peru, headed to Machu Picchu, Michelle reached back to me in Hawaii by email and asked me to let go of the idea of completing the final chapter of this book just until she got back from her trip, so she could focus on her spiritual pilgrimage. We felt we were so close to having this book completed, but that final ending would have to wait; and I agreed. Our conscious minds had forgotten it was already done!

When Michelle returned home, we talked about her trip to Peru and this final chapter of our book. Michelle was energetic and upbeat, feeling in touch with her heart, mind, and soul, her power, her mana, God, and the Universe. She was excited to return home to her children who had been staying with their father, Michelle's now former husband.

To her surprise, it had sounded like the children had spent much of the two weeks not only with their father, but also with his new girlfriend. Michelle was in Peru for just two weeks, and suddenly the new girlfriend seemed to be deeply entrenched in her children's lives.

I was tempted to spin out just hearing this, but Michelle was steadfast that...

Living spin-free puts you on the road to being truly
healthy and happy
in all of your relationships.

Michelle was not angry or hurt; instead she felt unsettled and uneasy with how suddenly this new relationship moved along while she was gone. Thanks to life in the garden, Michelle didn't spin out at all; she simply floated downstream. She was cordial and polite with the girlfriend present at all the kids' activities that weekend.

He had been dating, so the fact that he had a new girlfriend did not hit her heartstrings. It was just too much too fast; the girlfriend was text messaging the kids on Michelle's phone how much she loves them, and buying the children gifts. It was an unexpected express train that was now on the horizon of her children's lives.

So, thanks to her dedication to mana gardening, there were only a few uncomfortable minutes that we talked about this surprising manifestation; minutes where (even though we are the ones who wrote this book) we forgot a major lesson of the garden!

While we fully recognized that Michelle was right by choosing to float downstream and not spin out, we both completely forgot to move our thoughts inward first so Michelle could figure out what she really wanted. Fortunately, we caught ourselves less than 20 minutes into this detour from what we learned with mana gardening.

In those 20 minutes I kept making outward-focused suggestions, like: "Well, you could do this. You could do that. That is what I would want to do..."

All of my suggestions had an emotional edge to them, but Michelle said, "Nope. I'm not going to do any of those things, because all of them are reactionary, and I feel that is absolutely the wrong way to step."

We were talking it out and wasting all of our happiness on the old way of dealing with problems! Michelle just needed to go to the garden, because she had to find out what she really wanted. I was disappointed in myself for wasting even a few minutes of our precious happy time on thinking about what she didn't want, like, or enjoy, rather than on what she did want!

This was the turning point for everything—the understanding that mana gardening skills have to become our habit—*completely*. Still, after all that we have learned, after all the sweet new skills that we had gained, I was still capable of doing things the old way almost as a reflex.

In this detour to the old ways of facing concerns, Michelle was much better at not getting into the old patterns than I was. She was steadfast in saying to my reactionary suggestions, "I don't know what I want, but I know I don't like how this or that would make me feel." Once we acknowledged that she needed to go within to figure out what she really wanted, she caught herself and reminded me that...

Your happiness is based solely on you and you must look inward
and decide on your own what that picture will be.

Michelle got off the phone, began using the no-spin power tool, and asked herself what she wanted. She sought a concise answer without emotion. She told me later that day that she heard very clearly exactly what she wanted in a concise sentence that could be repeated to her former husband in a way that would make her feel neither inferior nor superior, and in a way that would not trigger either of them. It was an absolutely brilliant sentence from the garden that she did repeat to him the very next day.

She wanted the kids to have some time with just their dad, and she wanted at least some of the children's activities to be shared only with parents. The next day she said what she wanted plainly and without asking for any discussion. They both agreed to her simple request, and she was able to let go and move on. Even if they had disagreed—at that moment she felt satisfied that she knew what she wanted and had the strength to express it! She felt empowered.

Consistent mana gardening taught us to pay attention to those moments when we feel unsettled, uneasy, or uncomfortable without allowing those feelings and associated thoughts to take us down into an emotional spin. Don't just disregard those moments. When you feel unsettled like that, your body is telling you something. Those feelings were telling Michelle she had a bit of inner work to do surrounding the situation. Focus on your inner paradise, take all the stuff circling around in your head, and intend to reduce it to a sentence that states clearly, concisely, and without emotion, what it is you really want.

The fact is, though Michelle and I enter our inner gardens daily, we still have moments where we forget to use our tools. Yet when we turn ourselves around and get back in the garden, we get back to finding real answers.

It has helped us tremendously to have friends we can confide in who practice mana gardening. Whenever we don't know what we really want, whenever we are stalling on resolving issues, when we catch ourselves beginning to spin out, or trying to work through things with another person without doing our own personal work first, we remind each other to get back in the garden and reflect inward.

Even without a friend who participates, this mindset is helpful for everyone we love as we try to direct them away from adding to or fueling emotionally charged issues. We are now encouraging those we love to first take the time to find out what they want. My husband understands these skills, because it is the Hawaiian way, but because of his stroke, it is often challenging for him to focus on what he wants. Through practicing this ancient Hawaiian technique, I learned to behave as if things are already markedly better for him. My change in perspective seems contagious, and when I cannot navigate others toward choosing the paths I found, I rely on the knowledge that...

Imagining things as being better can actually improve your life emotionally and physically.

With or without a friend who plays with mana gardening, these concepts can give you a foundation for living in and creating healthy relationships. For Michelle and me, it took all our lives up to now to recognize that many of the skills we were taught before don't work. The key to this final chapter, as Michelle and I realized, is that from now on, we have to be focused toward creating new beneficial habits and patterns that steer us clear from our old, ineffective habits of coping and reacting.

With consistent mana gardening, you, too, will understand that the center of your soul has to be the starting point for everything. It is at that moment we want you to remember that...

All the wisdom of Mana Gardening is only
valuable if you use it.

We were searching for only one thing: the key to happiness. Like so many before us who set out on this same path, we came to understand that everything we were looking for was already within us. We simply needed to find a way inward that worked for us.

Through mana gardening, which is simply a new path to ancient wisdom taught centuries ago, we discovered a way to park our thoughts in heaven, relax effortlessly, and identify what happiness meant to us personally. What was surprising was that it not only offered us a way to change our perspectives in regards to the future, but also a way to change our perspectives of the past!

Discovering and practicing this method changed the way we approach everything we do and, through these experiences, we realized a beautiful way to truly live happily. We shared our experiences to enrich the lives of our children and all who seek happiness. We believe that, in taking this new lifestyle to heart, lasting happiness can be yours and you can live a better life, too.

We suggest that you put his book someplace where you will pass by it each and every day of your life. Put your hand on it when you pass by it. Do this to remind yourself to start from within, enter your personal paradise, your sacred inner garden, every time you have a moment to spare. Keep the snippets page with you too, make copies and place them where you will see them every day to remind yourself to get in your garden. If you continue to practice mana gardening, you will begin to discover an ancient wisdom that can empower you deep from within. This energy, this mana, will fill your life with more laughter and more joy than you thought possible and, in mastering this, that ever-flowing sense of happiness will always be within reach.

See you in the garden.

MAKANA:

Take a moment to email yourself one of your favorite mana gardening experiences.

Send a copy to us if you would like it to be considered for inclusion in our upcoming book, Journeys Within: a Compilation of Mana Gardening Experiences from Around the World.

Submit your experience via the Contact Us form at www.managardening.com

Snippets

We've included two sets of Mana Gardening wisdom. We invite you to tear out these pages and make copies of them. Keep a copy with you and place others where you will see them every day to remind yourself to spend time *Mana Gardening*.

There is a simple way to tap into lifelong inner strength and happiness.

True happiness is independent of everything and everyone around you.

The only thing in life we truly have the power to change is our perspective.

Visualize your idea of paradise and allow yourself to be there.

Let your active mind relax in your paradise,
far from the world around you.

Mana Gardening reveals how you perceive the people in
your life and identifies
the depth in which you value and trust them.

To love and be loved in a relationship, each person
must be *in*
and willing to let each other in, always.

Knowing what you want allows you to make things
better in your life.

Mana Gardening can only show to others what you
truly feel ready to reveal.

Whenever the chaos of life is pushing your buttons…
float downstream…
and let it all go.

You can erase and replace unbeneficial memories
to strengthen yourself
emotionally and physically.

To experience a spiritual connection in your life,
welcome Divine presence from within.

Living spin-free puts you on the road to being truly
healthy and happy
in all of your relationships.

Your happiness is based solely on you and you must look
inward
and decide on your own what that picture will be.

The mental imagery of Mana Gardening can activate the
brain and body as if physical things
are really happening.

Imagining things as being better can actually improve
your life emotionally and physically.

All the wisdom of Mana Gardening is only
valuable if you use it.

SNIPPETS

There is a simple way to tap into lifelong inner strength and happiness.

True happiness is independent of everything and everyone around you.

The only thing in life we truly have the power to change is our perspective.

Visualize your idea of paradise and allow yourself to be there.

Let your active mind relax in your paradise,
far from the world around you.

Mana Gardening reveals how you perceive the people in
your life and identifies
the depth in which you value and trust them.

To love and be loved in a relationship, each person
must be *in*
and willing to let each other in, always.

Knowing what you want allows you to make things
better in your life.

Mana Gardening can only show to others what you
truly feel ready to reveal.

Whenever the chaos of life is pushing your buttons…
float downstream…
and let it all go.

You can erase and replace unbeneficial memories
to strengthen yourself
emotionally and physically.

To experience a spiritual connection in your life,
welcome Divine presence from within.

Living spin-free puts you on the road to being truly
healthy and happy
in all of your relationships.

Your happiness is based solely on you and you must look
inward
and decide on your own what that picture will be.

The mental imagery of Mana Gardening can activate the
brain and body as if physical things
are really happening.

Imagining things as being better can actually improve
your life emotionally and physically.

All the wisdom of Mana Gardening is only
valuable if you use it.

REFERENCES

1. Malouin F, Richards CL, Durand A, et al. Effects of practice, visual loss, limb amputation and disuse on motor imagery vividness. *Neurorehabil Neural Repair.* 2009; 23:449–463.

2. Guillot A, Collet C, Nguyen VA, Malouin F, Richards C, et al. Brain activity during visual versus kinesthetic imagery: an fMRI study. *Hum Brain Mapp.* 2009;30: 2157–2172.

3. Guillot A, Collet C, Nguyen VA, Malouin F, Richards C, et al. Functional neuroanatomical networks associated with expertise in motorimagery. *Neuroimage.* 2008;41:1471–1483.

4. Mihara M, Miyai I, Hattori N, Hatakenaka M, Yagura H, Kawano T, Okibayashi M, Danjo N, Ishikawa A, Inoue Y, Kubota K. Neurofeedback using real-time near-infrared spectroscopy enhances motor imagery related cortical activation. *PLoS One.* 2012;7(3):e32234.

5. Ruby P, Decety J. Effect of subjective perspective taking during simulation of action: a PET investigation of agency. *Nat Neurosci.* 2001;4:546–550.

6. Gerardin E, Sirigu A, Lehericy S, Poline JB, Gaymard B, et al. Partially overlapping neural networks for real and imagined hand movements. *Cereb Cortex.* 2000;10:1093–1104.

7. deCharms RC, Christoff K, Glover GH, Pauly JM, Whitfield S, et al. Learned regulation of spatially localized brain activation using real-time fMRI. *Neuroimage.* 2004;21:436–443.

8. Lotze M, Halsband U. Motor imagery. *J Physiol Paris.* 2006;99:386–395.

9. Malouin F, Richards CL. Mental practice for relearning locomotor skills. *Phys Ther.* 2010;90(2):240-51.

10. Malouin F, Richards CL, Jackson PL, et al. Brain activations during motor imagery of locomotor-related tasks: a PET study. *Hum Brain Mapp.* 2003;19:47–62.

11. Subramanian L, Morris MB, Brosnan M, Turner DL, Morris HR, Linden DE. Functional magnetic resonance imaging neurofeedback-guided motor imagery training and motor training for Parkinson's disease: randomized trial. *Front Behav Neurosci.* 2016;10:111.

12. Marins TF, Rodrigues EC, Engel A, et al. Enhancing motor network activity using real-time functional MRI neurofeedback of left premotor cortex. *Front Behav Neurosci.* 2015;9:341.

13. Szameitat AJ, Shen S, Sterr A. Motor imagery of complex everyday movements: an fMRI study. *Neuroimage.* 2007;34:702–713.

14. Jackson PL, Lafleur MF, Malouin F, et al. Potential role of mental practice using motor imagery in neurological rehabilitation. *Arch Phys Med Rehabil.* 2001;82:1133–1141.

15. Decety J, Perani D, Jeannerod M, Bettinardi V, Tadary B, et al. Mapping motor representations with positron emission tomography. *Nature.* 1994;371:600–602.

16. Decety J, Jeannerod M, Germain M, Pastene J. Vegetative responses during imagined movement is proportional to mental effort. *Behav Brain Res.* 1991:42:1–5.

17. Wuyam B, Moosavi SH, Decety J, et al. Imagination of dynamic exercise produced ventilatory responses which were more apparent in competitive sportsmen. *J Physiol.* 1995;482:713–724.

18. Fusi S, Cutuli D, Valente MR, et al. Cardioventilatory responses during real or imagined walking at low speed. *Arch Ital Biol*. 2005;143:223–228.

19. Sacco K, Cauda F, Cerliani L, et al. Motor imagery of walking following training in locomotor attention: the effect of "the tango lesson." *Neuroimage*. 2006;32:1441–1449.

20. Dickstein R, Deutsch JE. Motor imagery in physical therapist practice. *Phys Ther*. 2007;87:942–953.

21. Slimani M, Taylor L, Baker JS, Elleuch A et al. Effects of mental training on muscular force, hormonal and physiological changes in kickboxers. *J Sports Med Phys Fitness*. 2016 Jul 5.

22. Murphy SM. Imagery interventions in sport. *Med Sci Sports Exerc*. 1994;26:486–494.

23. Guillot A, Moschberger K, Collet C. Coupling movement with imagery as a new perspective for motor imagery practice. *Behav Brain Funct*. 2013;Feb 20;9(1):8.

24. Moran A, Guillot A, Macintyre T, Collet C. Re-imagining motor imagery: building bridges between cognitive neuroscience and sport psychology. *Br J Psychol*. 2012;103(2):224-47.

25. Anema HA, de Haan AM, Gebuis T, Dijkerman HC. Thinking about touch facilitates tactile but not auditory processing. *Exp Brain Res*. 2012; 218(3):373-80.

26. Polage DC. Fabrication inflation increases as source monitoring ability decreases. *Acta Psychol*. 2012;139(2):335-42.

27. Scoboria A, Mazzoni G, Jarry JL, Bernstein DM. Personalized and not general suggestion produces false autobiographical memories and suggestion-consistent behavior. *Acta Psychol*. 2012;139(1):225-32.

28. Konorski J. Conditioned Reflexes and Neuron Organization. Cambridge: Cambridge University Press. (1948) p 134.

29. Kaptchuk TJ, Friedlander E, Kelley JM, Sanchez MN, et al. Placebos without Deception: A Randomized Controlled Trial in Irritable Bowel Syndrome. *PLoS ONE.* 2010;5 (12):e15591.

30. Miller FG, Colloca L, Kaptchuk TJ. The placebo effect: illness and interpersonal healing. *Perspec Biol Med.* 2009;52:518–39.

31. Flik CE, Bakker L, Laan W, van Rood YR, et al. Systematic review: The placebo effect of psychological interventions in the treatment of irritable bowel syndrome. *World J Gastroenterol.* 2017;23(12):2223-2233.

32. Benson H, McCallie DP. Angina pectoris and the placebo effect. *N Engl J of Med.* 1979;300 (25):1424–9.

33. Moseley JB, O'Malley K, Petersen NJ, et al. "A controlled trial of arthroscopic surgery for osteoarthritis of the knee". *N Engl J of Med.* 2002;347 (2): 81–8.

34. Ikemi Y, Nakagawa S. A psychosomatic study of contagious dermatitis. *Kyoshu J Med Sci* 1962;13:335–50.

35. O'Boyle DJ, Binns AS, Sumner JJ. On the efficacy of alcohol placebos in inducing feelings of intoxication. *Psychopharmacol.* 1994;115 (1–2):229–36.

36. Flaten MA, Simonsen T, Olsen H. Drug-related information generates placebo and nocebo responses that modify the drug response. *Psychosom Med.* 1999;61 (2):250–5.

37. Fillmore MT, Mulvihill LE, Vogel-Sprott M. "The expected drug and its expected effect interact to determine placebo responses to alcohol and caffeine". *Psychopharmacol.* 1994;115(3):383–8.

38. Kirsch I. Specifying non-specifics: Psychological mechanism of the placebo effect. The Placebo Effect: An Interdisciplinary Exploration. Cambridge: Harvard University Press. (1997) p. 166–86.

39. Buckalew LW, Ross S. Relationship of perceptual characteristics to efficacy of placebos. *Psychol Rep.* 1981;49 (3):955–61.

40. Price DD, Craggs J, Verne GN, Perlstein WM, Robinson ME. Placebo analgesia is accompanied by large reductions in pain-related brain activity in irritable bowel syndrome patients. *Pain.* 2007;127(1-2):63-72.

41. Kirsch I, Weixel LJ. Double-blind versus deceptive administration of a placebo. *Behav Neurosci,* 1988;102(2):319-323.

42. Keller PE. Mental imagery in music performance: underlying mechanisms and potential benefits. *Ann N Y Acad Sci.* 2012;1252:206-13.

43. "Introduction to Neuroplasticity." *MemoryZine.com.* Practical Memory Institute. 16 Nov. 2009. Web. 02 July 2010.

ACKNOWLEDGEMENTS

Aloha!

Above all, I want thank my beautiful children and grandchildren. You are, and always will be, all that is sweet in my life! I am so very proud of each and every one of you! To Llewellyn Kamalani, you are the perfect Yin to the Yang of my world and I love my life with you. To the people of the Hawaiian Kingdom, thank you for teaching me how to open my eyes to the true beauty in all that surrounds me. To my wonderful family and those who have shared my life, thank you for loving me throughout everything!

To Sally Frisbie, Carmen Campbell, Michelle Shine, and Renate Mainka-Waschlinger: thank you for your friendship, laughter, and devotion. To Michelle, thank you for always taking the high road, no matter what the cost to you personally. You are amazing! With love and reverence, I humbly thank You, Lord, for all that You have given me and for leading Michelle to my door to suggest we try this simple thing that we call Mana Gardening. To Mana Gardening, thank you for empowering me to LIVE FOR THE SILVER LINING!

Love, Keti

My deep appreciation goes to the many who supported and inspired me during the creation of this work. My gratitude abounds to T.G. Shen Ballesteros. Mahalo for explaining the ancient inner garden concept to me, for the guidance, and for your amazing spirit! See you at the inner garden waterfall, brother!

Mahalo nui loa and Aloha nui loa goes to you, Keti, for your willingness to try Mana Gardening with me, for your continued partnership in this endeavor, for your openness, your drive, your love and your deeply devoted friendship. To Llewellyn Kamalani, the love of Keti's life, thanks for always being the leader of the band! I want to thank my children for their sweet love and bright light, and for playing in the garden with me. I am particularly grateful to my dear friends and loving family and thank you all graciously for your love and support. I give special appreciation to my Mom, Stephanie Harris Root, Allison Blake, Joy Waters, Jon Handelman and Molly McClellan for your loving care and devotion.

I thank God, the Great Spirit, for leading me to the Mana Gardening concept, for the enlightening process of self-discovery, for teaching me to know and rely on my inner guidance, and for the high level of personal growth and fulfillment that has come with practicing this inner technique. Lastly, special appreciation goes to my sacred inner garden for all the relaxation, the guidance and intuition, the joy, the love and the *magic*!

With Love and Aloha, Michelle

About The Authors

Keti Kamalani and Michelle Shine, Ph.D. are cofounders of Mana Gardening® and Mana Gardening Institute.

Keti Kamalani has more than 20 years of professional research experience in cellular biology and tissue engineering. Her passion in the spiritual sense is based on personal experiences from life with her Native Hawaiian husband and time spent in over 40 countries. She is the Director of the Mana Gardening Institute, developer of Mana Gardening Yoga, and is a Certified Hatha Yoga Instructor. Keti and her family live on a farm in Hawaii where they enjoy writing and playing music.

Biomedical Scientist, **Michelle Shine,** has published in stem cell biology, tissue engineering, complementary and alternative medicine, cell signaling and microbiology. She gained a special passion for bridging science and spirituality while living amongst the immense natural beauty of southwestern Colorado. She enjoys music, surfing, hiking, and snowboarding. She lives in the Blue Ridge Mountains with two happy children sharing Mana Gardening skills and science worldwide as CEO and Director of Research for Mana Gardening Institute.

PHOTO CREDITS

All photos in this publication were used with permission.

Front cover photos from left to right:
Above Lanikai, Windward Oahu, Hawaii by Amanda Hibberd;
Hawaii Love, Makaha, Oahu, Hawaii by Amanda Hibberd;
Ko'olau Mountain Range around Kaneohe Bay, Oahu, Hawaii
by Michelle Shine; Hawaiian Sunset, North Shore Oahu,
Hawaii by Amanda Hibberd; Embracing the Universe at Machu
Picchu, Peru by Michelle Shine

Back cover photos from left to right:
Keti on the Farm, Windward Oahu, Hawaii by Lew Kamalani;
Michelle in the Sun, Asheville, North Carolina by
Michelle Shine

Chapter images:
Ch 1: Black-eyed Susans at Asheville Botanical Gardens,
Asheville, North Carolina by Michelle Shine

Ch 2: Doorway, Ollantaytambo, Peru by Michelle Shine

Ch 3: Mauna Wili Falls, Oahu, Hawaii by Michelle Shine

Ch 4: Echinacea Beauties in Fairview, North Carolina by
Michelle Shine

Ch 5: Love Orchids in Honolulu, Hawaii by Michelle Shine

Ch 6: The Flash Sunset, North Shore, Oahu, Hawaii by
Michelle Shine

Ch 7: Cluster Tomatoes in Asheville, North Carolina by
Michelle Shine

Ch 8: Peace at Fontana Lake, Joyce Kilmer Memorial Forest
Park, Graham County, North Carolina by Michelle Shine

Ch 9: Cool Tree, Windward Oahu, Hawaii by Keti Kamalani

Ch 10: Saqsaywaman Ruins, Cuzco, Peru by Michelle Shine

Ch 11: Intimate Orchids in Honolulu, Hawaii by Michelle Shine

Ch 12: Stone Heart, Machu Picchu, Peru by Michelle Shine

Ch 13: Craggy Garden Sunset, Craggy Gardens, Blue Ridge
National Heritage Area, near Asheville, North Carolina by
Michelle Shine

MANA
GARDENING®
INSTITUTE

Keti Kamalani and Michelle Shine, Ph.D. are thrilled to share the ancient Hawaiian wisdom of Mana Gardening with you. They are available for seminars, conferences, workshops, webinars, interviews, retreats, and private sessions. Mana Gardening® training is available online, via teleconference and in person.

Please visit online to find out about course offerings, learn more about using Mana Gardening every day, order books and products, read blogs, schedule, and subscribe.

WWW.MANAGARDENING.COM

Mana Gardening Institute, LLC is a Hawaii-based organization established to facilitate scientific research in forthright personal empowerment and Mana Gardening® techniques. Visit the website to learn more about our Mana Sciences™ and Mana Psychology™ research.

FOLLOW US:

FACEBOOK: facebook.com/ManaGardening

TWITTER: twitter.com/managardening

INSTAGRAM: instagram.com/managardening

Master Shen is available for personal training sessions by phone coaching. With 30+ years experience, Master Shen blends the energy, skill, and self-defense techniques of Chinese Internal Kung Fu with Ancient Hawaiian healing and spiritual wisdom to offer inspired solutions for life's challenges. Students receive immediate and valuable results, such as: stress reduction, emotional relaxation, and loving creativity for positive growth and bountiful blessings.

T.G. Shen Ballesteros
Aloha Nui Ohana (Family of Great Love)
P.O. Box 990, Makawao, HI 96768
Email: contribute@AlohaNuiOhana.com
www.AlohaNuiOahana.com